Conflict of Power

Conflict of Power

Sadie Belew

Library of Congress Control Number: 2009904881
ISBN: Hardcover   978-1-4415-3783-6
               Softcover   978-1-4415-3782-9

To order additional copies of this book, contact:
Xlibris Corporation
1-888-795-4274
www.Xlibris.com
Orders@Xlibris.com
59690

CONTENTS

PART 1:   The Economy and Campaign Attacks 15

PART 2:   Voters 20

PART 3:   President-elect Barack's Plans 24

PART 4:   Top Stories of 2008 31

PART 5:   Ups and Downs of the Transition 35

PART 6:   The Inauguration 43

PART 7:   The Presidency 46

PART 8:   The Theory 58

PART 9:   The American Dream 87

PART 10: The First Lady 90

To My Family and Friend

I acknowledge my husband
Larry Belew
For his help
My son
Danny Webster
For his support
My friend
Robert Wiley
For his support

Barack Obama
How did Barack Accomplish Victory?

PREFACE

For several years, I have been planning to write a book, but I could not decide what I actually wanted to write about. Suddenly, while watching a newscast about Barack, from within a still small voice seemed to whisper, "Write about Barack."

From the very "first" speech to the "last," I was held in high emotion. Such authority, power to create respect and confidence, I had never before perceived. This mysterious man I thought can actually become president of the *United States of America*!

I found myself absorbed in every speech and newscast. I defended him and was drawn to him for no reason that I can explain except the mystery lurking behind him. Others I know (family and friends) would call him a Muslim or say they didn't know if they could trust him. I stood by my belief that he is not a Muslim, and I have not been regretful. I rejoiced with millions of others when Barack won the election. I feel in my heart "he was and is" the best choice to lead this country forward.

SADIE BELEW

INTRODUCTION

The contents of this book is about the conflict going on in America's government and how Barack Obama wants to change the way a failed policy has dominated the economy for eight years.

Barack wants unity in government between countries and all nationalities. When unity prevails, there is success, people work together making decisions that work for a better future. America's economy depends on it; and when America experiences success, the famous statement, "Yes, we can!" will be as historical as the election of an African American.

Barack's acceptance speech, after his election, brought many people to their knees: tears flowed, shouts resounded in praises. Voters, ready for change, heard ideas and opinions that touched their heart and very soul.

Barack Obama cannot let the American people down. If he does, hope will be lost. A once thriving economy will hold only fear. There must be unity and a putting away of prejudicial opinions. In a time of economic fears, Barack offered hope, and he beat the odds.

PART 1

THE ECONOMY
AND CAMPAIGN ATTACKS

The economy can make or break businesses, create or destroy jobs. A good economy can make a country thrive and prosper. One can receive wealth in a time of economic driven market prosperity, but some people trust in their riches, and it is a false security that does not always last. They can be deceived and lose their wealth. The recent stock market slide downward was proof enough that wealth cannot always be counted on.

Some people get rich through hard work, others by being deceitful. Deceit makes a person believe something that is false. How many times are Americans fooled by TV ads that "promise" a product will work when in fact it doesn't. Our government also misleads for their own advantage. America is so far in debt. It will take a "miracle" to dig out all the debauchery, but we are one nation under God, and we believe in miracles.

During a time of economic distress, Barack ran an extraordinary campaign. He was able to raise an enormous amount of money at a time of economic troubles involving American people. He raised more money than any candidate in the history of the American presidency. His attitude gave him a good advantage among whites and a trust in his plan, but some whites thought he may support blacks at their expense. America pondered the question: is this the right point in time to elect a black president? Many voters questioned the truth of his story about change. There was much concern over it ever materializing. The economy must make a rebound and "strengthen" equal opportunity for all Americans.

A poor economy creates crime, a lost trust in a government that rewards the wealthy. Americans must fight crime and crack down on drugs that is destroying our youth.

America must provide a positive environment that ensures encouragement to all children. The direction children receive at home sets the course for their entire lives. Train a child in the way he should go, and when he is old, he will continue to follow the right path.

In ancient times the penalty for several crimes was capital punishment, so failing to properly control a child could indirectly lead to his death. Parents who ignore their children or fail to give them the discipline they need can cause them to have a dismal future. If you spare your child the necessary instruction he needs, you may well be teaching him hate. For many years now, discipline has taken the form of abuse, leading to the fact that children never learn that their actions carry consequences.

America has turned from our forefathers' principles of action: uprightness with honor, fundamental beliefs such as religious principles. For America to survive such an economic disaster, we must once again recognize and return to godly laws, such as marriage between a man and a woman. God made a woman to be a helpmate to her husband.

Barack won the primary election against Senator Hillary Clinton, a well-known former "first lady" who desperately wanted to be the first woman president. She was popular among white women voters. Barack knew he had to find a way to win over the women that voted for Hillary. Many women were angry and said they would vote for McCain.

Hillary hit the campaign trail "warning" women that to vote for McCain would be voting for the same Bush policy of government, a policy Democrats say has failed in the past.

Barack's selection of Joe Biden for vice president most certainly expressed leadership. The Delaware senator most likely increased the Democratic votes. Wise decisions are made with advice and some instruction from other wise candidates. Some of the basic qualities that help shape wise decisions include peace, humility, and a conciliatory attitude. Barack's speeches and actions had all of these qualities. He made the right decisions, listened to advice, was peaceful, humble, and has a conciliatory attitude. There was something almost "magical" about the way he won people over.

It was the right time in history for Barack to appear on America's timetable of events. Time for a man of "color" to hold the high rank of commander in chief. Time for a new beginning with possible worthy results. A time in history our children and grandchildren can read about and be proud Americans, not in the way of being "haughty" or "arrogant" but thinking well of oneself. Good character shows moral strength and will distinguish judicious facts.

The fact is America needs a ring of changes. Lawmakers need changeability and reform back to "God's Laws." They need to tell the atheists, "There is a God, and America will serve the only true God, creator and ruler of the world!"

If Barack will remember his promises and his dedication to helping the poor, a wise leader will become a wise president. Wisdom is eternal and brings meaning and joy to our lives.

Barack faced yet another uphill battle. Winning against John McCain, a Republican and a war hero. It was evident; the path would grow much larger and dangerous. The race was on, and the negative advertisements were spinning out of control.

The Muslim "attack" had voters in a frenzy. Barack did live in Indonesia and attend a predominantly Muslim school, but he is just African American. McCain hammered Barack on taxes, spending, and not being ready to become commander in chief. Higher taxes on the "wealthy" is Barack's agenda.

McCain and wife Cindy are "millionaires," own several homes, and do not have to fret about the economy. McCain's campaign message was Country First, the wrong words to a nation on the verge of destruction.

The socialism "attack" was not a surprise. McCain called Barack's tax plan "welfare." That must brand the bailout of Wall Street and the banks "welfare" also. Millionaires were losing millions, so Washington decided to meet, discuss issues and bail out Wall Street.

McCain dropped in the polls, brought up Barack's inexperience, his pastor Rev. Jeremiah Wright whose messages seemed to "attack" America. The news stations had a field day about Rev. Wright. They could not perceive how Barack could sit and listen to Rev. Wright for several years and not share his "views." It is very possible to be deceived. Satan is a "liar" and "deceiver" of all people.

William Ayers became a hot political topic. Barack was accused of "paling around" with a terrorist. Barack worked with Ayers several years after he was given the reputation of being a terrorist.

ACORN, an organization that helps voters to register, came under the Republican's fire. They blamed Barack for hiring the organization. It was true the organization's employees did commit crimes, but Barack only wanted to get unregistered voters registered. If one works hard, he may profit, but only talking will lead to poverty.

These negative "attacks" only turned voters off for such behavior is "childish" and "foolish." Slander is the spreading of false and damaging information about another person as if it were true. The wise person is able to hold their tongue and feed a compliment or words of encouragement to "motivate" a person who has long had a dream to fulfill. Our destiny sometimes lie in the way we speak.

Voters saw a presidential characteristic side of Barack as the campaign went forward. They saw new leadership and a uniter. Voters are hungry for unity, a oneness that joins in action and interest.

McCain's "huge" mistake was selecting Sarah Palin for vice president. She knew how to give a good speech, but the winking turned voters off. A signal to some voters that she thought by being "playful" she could win the debate against Senator Joe Biden, who is experienced in foreign affairs. During the debate his grin was "ear to ear." Palin was no match in foreign affairs, and he knew it. There was no way a governor from Alaska could hope to win against a long-standing Senator with Washington experience. It was apparent she had no knowledge of world affairs.

Palin put up a good fight against Barack and Joe Biden, but voters didn't see the experience or the plan she lay out in her speeches, the strength was missing.

On the campaign trail, the "attacks" on Barack became more intense because of William Ayers who is accused of being a terrorist against his own country. It prompted some voters into a rage, and a plot to assassinate Barack was broken up by law enforcement agents. This plot could have gone unnoticed and caused a great deal of pain and sorrow.

There was a message in their attacks that sent out an unfavorable content to many people who didn't really understand Barack or his message of change. It is very deceitful to spread false claims.

Former Secretary of State Colin Powell decided, "Enough is enough!" He saw a need for a change in government and endorsed Barack for president.

Sarah, being a woman, helped McCain draw larger crowds. Some voters, especially men, were drawn to her. Some women voters wanted a woman regardless of her experience. She was criticized repeatedly by the media. They said she was not qualified if something should happen to McCain. A woman vice president at this time was not on God's timetable. God has "appointed" times for all world occurrences. Jesus,

God's only son, came into the world at the exact appointed time set by God. He came to save his people from their sins and claim them for his own. God's wisdom cannot be compared to a foolish and corrupt nation that has disobeyed the laws he has set forth.

Barack's message of change strengthened. America was on the brink of another "Great Depression," but will change only bring an increase to the deficit, more jobs lost, and higher taxes? America has a half-billion-dollar deficit, considered to be the highest in U.S. history. Many investors became alarmed and retreated from stocks, retirement funds and took huge hits. Voters heard promises for a better America, which previously seemed out of sight. Those promises offered "hope," and the American people have faith. That faith dwells in a "great" nation that has fought many wars, suffered a depression, but still lives on and will never die. The world is watching. America must not close her eyes to the truth and be a force once more to make a difference.

Hopefully, Barack's message will not only be successful but will bring people together in a way that will produce change in many hearts that have grown cold. Government needs to change their way of thinking and find a way to get along, stop acting like children that have not been taught rules to go by.

Voters saw many childish ways and heard hateful words in this campaign that they had not seen or heard before. Voters were getting disgusted and discouraged through the whole process. Barack offered a change from all the silly "attacks" that took place in the campaign. It will be remembered in history as a degrading way to achieve success.

PART 2

VOTERS

V oters from every state were "anxious" and "excited" about the election. First-time voters were flocking like birds to register. TV ads, calls, and door-to-door visits helped to get the message across the nation. This election was going to make history. The first ever African American president or the first woman vice president.

False opinions "floated" from person to person. The Internet was filled with falsehood. Rumors such as "Barack is the Antichrist!" The Antichrist will be the great "enemy" or "opponent" of Christ. He will imitate Christ in regard to "signs" and miraculous occurrences. In order to imitate, one has to be like that person. Christ was a Jew; the Antichrist will have to be a Jew. He will be empowered by Satan. Satan imitates God. A rumor from the Internet: Barack will bring the Antichrist into the world scene. The Antichrist is supposed to rise at a time of world disasters never before seen, with men running to and fro, facing problems that they do not know how to solve. This will be days distressful even to the elect. This dictator will probably fool many unlearned people not educated in Bible scripture. *Anti* means person opposed to some plan or idea. He will oppose everything concerning Christianity. The whole world will be under his rule.

Many unlearned people make mistaken assumptions and tend to assume the worst outcome of unusual events. No one can know God's "divine timing" or stop his "divine plan" for the entire world. God has all wisdom and cannot be considered secondary.

God with all his wisdom appoints world leaders to accomplish his will and creates disasters to make known that he alone rules the world.

World leaders throughout history were led by God's divine power. The Holy Spirit, third person of the Trinity, raises up leaders today.

Voters were ready for change, and change was (and is) Barack's message. After eight long years of the Bush administration, two wars, a bankrupt economy, America needed a change; however, Bush deserves credit for keeping America safe.

Barack must gain voters' respect, "differentiate" world affairs, and keep America safe. A duty not easy for any president. He will more than likely be popular with some voters and unpopular with others. There will always be different opinions between white voters and black voters. Those opinions, however, should never attack someone's character. God knows one's heart and can cause that person to rise or fall.

The last few weeks of the campaign, McCain and Palin became desperate, referring to themselves as "mavericks," an animal not marked with an owner's brand. They referred to Barack as a "rock star" because of the unusual large crowds he was able to draw. A rock star "sings and plays" rock music. This did not apply to Barack because he did not "perform or behave" like a performer.

The presidential race tightened after the final debate. White voters and GOP-leaning voters drifted back to the Republican's side. Barack shifted into overdrive, intending to spend the final two weeks campaigning in Republican states. He made a good case against the Republican party with his policy of change.

The Democratic campaign raised a million and a half dollars in September, passing the old record one month earlier. The support came from voters who expected a change in Washington and were excited about Barack's message.

Just three days left to make a case against Barack, Sen. John McCain focused on patriotism. It was clear to McCain that time was running out. He was "desperate" and wanted to win the race for the Republicans.

Reason: it was all about winning the war in Iraq. A war that cost America thousands of lives, billions of dollars, and a weak economy while the oil-rich countries accumulate a "surplus" of wealth! McCain, a war hero from the Vietnam War era, was beaten repeatedly, bones broken and lived in a small cell. It was a senseless war America could not win. Being a war hero does not make one "clever" enough to be a leader. A leader has integrity, compassion, and a personality that drives them forward. America wants victory in Iraq, but it is time for leaders of Iraq to take responsible actions.

Voters in all states were in high anticipation, pondering the question, who will win the White House? There was a surge in voters' registration statewide. Large gains were seen among blacks. They were voting for Barack to be the first African American to receive the honor of becoming president of the United States.

State officials had to watch for voting "abuses" that often occurs when there is a surge of new voters. It is a challenge for officials to make sure all machines are functioning and adequate. Some people had to wait for hours in the rain that stretched down streets and around city blocks. Some machines malfunctioned, and voters ended up having to use paper ballots.

Voters in the South voted mostly Republican, but across the United States, McCain and Barack were quite even. The youth voted for Barack and most of the independents. This was a race that took a lot of strength and intellect on both sides, and a winner could not be determined until all the votes were counted.

Voters had enthusiasm, and it was on Barack's side. Almost six in ten of his voters said they were excited about him becoming president and what he will accomplish. Speculations have him trying very hard to fulfill his campaign promises. When and if they are fulfilled can one truly say, "Yes, we can!" We can and we will with the help of a Great God and a government that "works" for the people.

Barack won the election, and McCain gave a great speech as he conceded the race. He remarked on the contest as being long and difficult, how Barack put up a good fight and deserves respect for his success. McCain was polite throughout the speech, and many people cheered his remarks but felt very sad.

Barack inspired millions of people to get out and vote. This act alone won him a large landslide, which was unexpected by many voters. Most news stations had Barack and McCain "neck and neck" in the polls. Polls are not always accurate and should not be counted as such.

Tuesday, November 4, 2008, America made history. The first African American was elected president of the United States of America! Who can say, "Dreams don't come true." This was a dream in the making for Barack when he was only a child.

How successful Barack is depends to a great extent how much the country supports him. The Senate and Congress must come together in a manner "acceptable" in decision making. Settling something beyond question will require "ability" to lead. Barack has displayed signs of "great" leadership that should correct an economy in a "tailspin" downward. He must fulfill his promises on Iraq, Afghanistan, healthcare, and alternative energy.

The time is now for America to be independent of the big oil companies. They are making billions in profit while the poor and middle class citizens are losing their homes and barely able to buy food. All the signs of a weak economy should wake up America's government and bring them to a plan acceptable to all involved.

The economy has driven up gas prices, and American car companies are going bankrupt. They must be saved from destruction and again be leaders in the auto industry. America should not have to be dependent on foreign car companies that have invaded our territory with cheap products. Some lawmakers have different ideas and want the American car companies to go bankrupt. To be dependent on foreign auto companies would be the same as being dependent on foreign oil. America is very gullible with a tendency to be easily deceived. America should keep jobs here in the United States and be completely independent of foreign countries. One of Barack's promises is to do just that, keep jobs where they belong, in the United States. Hopefully, he will keep his word, and America will once again be productive

Unemployment keeps climbing and more layoffs are expected in the future. These layoffs will likely be in hotels and restaurants. People cannot afford the high prices of a vacation or eating out.

PART 3

PRESIDENT-ELECT BARACK'S PLANS

Barack Obama, an intellect even as a small child, had a desire to be president. Born to a white mother and a black father at a time in history that would be impossible. He knew exactly what he wanted and set out to make it happen. As a child, he must have had an enormous battle raging inside—his father's abandonment, his racial identity, and his seeking to belong. The strength and courage he possesses, the politeness and the uncanny way he has "manageability," is beyond our imagination. From the streets of Chicago to the Senate, he apparently had a plan. The economic downturn in such a "disturbed" and "stormy" condition seemed hopeless. He saw the right time to carry out his dream of becoming president and remembered his book, *The Audacity of Hope*. Hope is similar to faith. *Hope* means a feeling that what one desires will happen. *Faith* means believing without proof. Barack's dream had precedence and accelerated into action that led to the White House.

Mr. President, Barack Obama, "destined" and led by the hand of God to become the first African American president. Will he bow down to the power of Washington or become the "greatest" American president in U.S. history? The future of a great nation depends on his leadership.

The sun is going down over the horizon, and darkness lies beneath. Barack must climb a steep mountain and turn darkness into light. A light filled with hope of a better future. What is to come will affect one's children and grandchildren.

People of "faith" must pray, not only for him but that America will move forward, put away prejudicial opinions and not "fear" a black president. Maybe in time, we can see each other "equally" and not judge one because of "color" or background.

In Barack's victory speech, he said, "Even if you didn't vote for me, I will still be your president." Those are words well spoken. Americans spoke with their votes, and it rang loud and clear that Barack would be their president. We are Americans with freedom of speech and the right to vote.

We the people should commend the Northern and Western states on their ability to perceive the truth and put away race issues. The Southern states should get over losing the Civil War. Christians should live what they preach, put aside "differences," and accept the fact we are all human beings.

Dr. Martin Luther King Jr. and his speeches live on, and the black race has been set free once again to pursue what was impossible. His "dream" is now reality, a fact that cannot be disregarded. Whites and blacks should walk "hand" in "hand" through distress and difficult times with heartfelt interest, not playing blame games or being prejudice.

President Bush wants a "smooth" transition and a "peaceful" transfer to take place between him and Barack. After the election, Bush invited Barack and Michelle to the White House and gave them a tour around the Rose Garden. The roses released their sweet fragrance as the president and president-elect discussed foreign policy. Foreign policy is a subject that requires a lot of concentration and a willing mind to work out all the details.

Plans to revive the economy was Barack's first priority; and the stock market took a swing upward after he announced Timothy Geithner, president of the New York Federal Reserve, as his treasury secretary. Swift action for a stimulus plan could aid states to provide health care, fund roads, and provide food stamps for the poor. Barack thinks the economy will get worse before getting better and has concerns about creating jobs over the high deficit. The deficit can elevate even higher as the problems are being taken seriously and more money needed to jump-start the economy. Barack wants to create at least two and a half million jobs very soon and get people back to work. He realizes the economy is at a critical point for all Americans.

Barack is determined to defeat Al Qaeda, who considers the United States an enemy oppressor. Al Qaeda made the remark that they fear the new president and compared him to "honorable black Americans."

The news video prompted Barack to select his national security team, fearing there could be an attack during the White House transition. Osama bin Laden is worried Barack will stamp out Al Qaeda once and for all as he vowed to do by sending more troops to Afghanistan. Now why would Al Qaeda fear Barack Obama if he is a "Muslim" as portrayed during the campaign? Al-Zawahri calls him an enemy of Al Qaeda. The Muslim's hate for America is simply because America supports Israel. Their intentions are to "destroy" the Jews, God's "chosen" people. God, who has all authority, will not let the descendants of Israel cease to be a nation. America must never turn her back on a land "chosen" by God and "given" to the Jews.

Jews and blacks have a common factor. Jews were held by Pharaoh as slaves. Pharaoh saw the Israelites as free labor to achieve his ambitions. God hardened Pharaoh's heart, and we Americans must guard our hearts, defend our nation and protect our values while supporting Israel.

Barack's demeanor is all about hope, not hate, which leads to war and destructive habits. He understands the real threat and wants to combat a real and dangerous enemy. America will never forget 9-11 or how our attackers' murderous actions took American lives on American soil. Barack recognizes the importance of winning the war in Afghanistan where the enemy hides and regroups. He understands that Iran wants to destroy the nation of Israel. Though one's wish is for world peace, the fact is nation will rise against nation and kingdom against kingdom for there will not be a perfect and permanent "peaceful world" until the return of the perfect "Prince of Peace"—the *Lord Jesus Christ*. "Behold, I am coming soon! My reward is with me, and I will give to everyone according to what he has done." This should tell the world that the Lord is the only way to have peace in such times of trouble.

Barack has some remarkable plans to strengthen America's security, such as a stronger military, protecting our chemical plants, and guarding our borders. America cannot tolerate terrorists seeking out their "targets" and committing murder. Terrorism has become a worldwide problem, and we face a new kind of security challenge, a challenge that we cannot ignore. Nuclear weapons are a worldwide concern and a threat that has increased. Barack wants to prevent the spread of nuclear weapons that poses an aggressive threat. Iran must be prevented from becoming a nuclear power. If Iran should "possess" nuclear weapons, it would be a disaster for Israel and every country worldwide.

December 1, 2008, Barack nominated Senator Hillary Rodham Clinton for secretary of state. Hillary is wife of the "former" president Bill Clinton. There are many questions being raised about the former president's international involvement.

Three former campaign rivals were selected by Barack to work with his team and help put issues in place. The three are New Mexico's Bill Richardson, Joe Biden, and Hillary Clinton. Joe Biden is vice president-elect, Hillary Clinton, the next secretary of state. Richardson withdrew his nomination for reasons concerning the government.

Barack is telling America that he is putting the country first, that he unites and is not a divider. When one unites, one does not hold a grudge against one's rival or attackers for a prudent man overlooks an insult.

The governors of the nation met with Barack to discuss his infrastructure-spending program. The money would go toward bridges, roads, and rail lines in the hopes of creating jobs and bringing the economy out of recession. Barack promised to move quickly on a stimulus package that he realizes the American people need to keep them from having to struggle to meet their debts and growing needs. The Republican governor's opinions at the meeting were taken into consideration as were the Democratic governors. The person who maintains only surface relationships with a wide number of people may eventually face ruin for lack of good advice when it is really needed because an unfriendly man pursues selfish ends. He defies all sound judgment.

The media had Barack's message of change completely wrong, asking, "Where's the change?" It is obvious Barack's message meant change in the way Washington operates, not change in experienced representatives.

Barack will take office January 20, 2009. He wants to combine experience with fresh thinking, and he defended his administration by saying the vision comes from him. The "collapse" of several banks and the financial markets were issues that keep him from working on his plans for the new administration. The economy was sinking fast, the pressure heightened to a strong point in Barack's mind causing him to react with assertion. Time was running out, and action was needed immediately. Barack had said we have one president at a time, but the constant need for a plan to revive the economy gave him an authority to speak on behalf of the American people.

The year 2008 will be remembered as a time of economic woes, millions of jobs have been lost and Barack sees an urgent need to create two and a half million jobs to save the economy from sinking even further into a crisis. November had the worst job loss in thirty-four years. Democratic leaders saw the evidence in the report that a huge spending program is needed at the cost of a massive national debt. Taxpayers are worried about passing the huge debt on to the next generation to reduce the mound of debts.

America has been in a long recession, and it could last two more years or longer. It is a downturn that mimics the Great Depression of the 1930s. *The* Great Depression was a hardship for many people. The economy was down; many people were laid off from their jobs. There was a shortage of food, making it necessary to form soup lines.

Some lawmakers want an economic plan in the billions. Democratic leaders want to have the plan ready to take affect after Barack takes office. Barack announced that he wants people to have patience as his administration tries to solve the issues facing America.

Organized labor helped elect Barack, and he promised them he would help in supporting their ideas of turning the companies around. Union membership has declined for reasons that pertain to jobs being outsourced and having to pay dues workers think is unrelated to their job. Barack thinks too many jobs are being outsourced to other countries and are taking American jobs from the United States. Companies currently get tax breaks for sending jobs to other countries where labor is found to be cheaper than in the United States. After Barack takes office, the tax breaks need to be brought before the lawmakers and ended.

The Big Three auto companies completed their plans on how to restructure and submitted them to Congress, replying the focus has to accomplish a swift economic rebound as opposed to a contract. The billions they are asking for will help workers to keep their jobs and retirement.

Congress should act quickly on a bailout plan for the auto industry before President-elect Barack Obama takes office, but they remain deeply divided on the rescue bailout plan. The members of Congress need to take into consideration the American car companies were started in the United States.

Many Republicans and some Democrats thought one or more auto companies should go bankrupt and then restructure, but under bankruptcy laws it would be difficult, and the collapse could eliminate millions of jobs. The chain reaction it would cause in many areas of employment would be a destruction in an economy already failing to meet the needs of the American people. American auto companies deserve to recover and be productive once again.

The automakers had to get down on their hands and knees and beg Congress for a bailout and promise to change their operations for federal assistance. GM made the remark the company could not survive without a huge bailout and could drag the entire industry down.

The three auto companies were seeking billions from the government to help them get through the economic crisis. Their sales were considered the worst for more than twenty-five years.

Without help from Congress, the suppliers will go bankrupt and would affect the foreign auto companies' sales. These foreign automakers have just about forced American auto companies to disappear from their own country. American people should take it as a warning and buy American products.

Republican lawmakers were "uncertain" about helping the American auto companies. They want a guarantee that taxpayers are protected and long-term competitiveness ensured, but how can taxpayers be assured protection when they are the ones in the long run paying for such a huge bailout. The Republicans were not "wary" of helping the banks and agreed on billions for insurance companies.

The Republicans insisted they were trying to help the companies and shield them from vigorous competition by letting them restructure.

The United Automobile Workers refused to accept the demands put forth by the Republicans because the current contract had not expired. Republicans wanted swift wage cuts that the UAW was willing to make in 2011. The billion-dollar bailout collapsed in the Senate.

Congress, unwilling to approve the bailout, decided it should be handed over to the Bush administration who declared it would prevent the "collapse" of the U.S. auto industry and thousands of jobs. Bush has the power to help these companies and prevent the economy from a further downturn.

U.S. auto companies employ thousands of workers, and thousands more produce the materials and parts. If one auto company goes under, job losses could be in the millions. This is a staggering fact and needs to be avoided. Most people recognize the auto companies are in a bad situation.

All of this information seems to indicate Republicans are against unionized companies that pays a "fair wage." The lack of "concern" for the economy and millions of job losses put America's government to shame. If you falter in times of trouble, your strength is very small.

Meanwhile, America's economy is in a deep recession. The failure to get a deal on the bailout upset markets. Some investors became upset and saw it as a sign the economy would not recover, and it prompted them to pull their money out of the stock market. Everything was up in the air, and as a result, the only policy was to wait and see what the government would do next.

Vehicle sales all across the world were losing demand for production. The "signs" were beginning to show a decline in Japanese sales. The automakers were dealing with the same crisis as the U.S. automakers, and the bad news was for Toyota and Honda since they are sold in North America. The economy will affect different companies around the world unless a change comes soon to boost the economic conditions.

Barack made a commitment to free America from dependence on foreign oil and find ways to create alternative energy technologies. America needs to be competitive with foreign countries in all-new technology. Barack has the confidence that America can rise above divisions and solve any problem that may loom ahead. This dark time in history can be a challenge to create new plans and ideas to pass down to the next generation.

Democrats and Republicans need to put away their differences and pass the economic plan. People need to get back to work, so they don't have to stay awake at night wondering if they will have money to pay their bills. There is not an easy way to fix this problem that is bogging down the economy.

Barack must wait until he takes office to carry out his plans. In the meantime Americans everywhere are losing their homes and retirement. Americans voted for the president-elect and believe that he will carry out the plans in the near future.

PART 4

TOP STORIES OF 2008

P resident Bush decided to take a break from all the problems of the economy and the bailout of the automakers. He visited Iraq and Afghanistan a few days before Barack takes office. Bush wanted to celebrate the U.S.-Iraq security agreement. U.S. troops are to withdraw from Iraq in 2011. The celebration turned out to be more like a nightmare that Bush was not expecting to happen on an overseas trip.

A surprise came from an Iraqi reporter who flung his shoes and barely missed President Bush. The shoes flew past Bush as he ducked, and there was a stunned look on his face that portrayed embarrassment. Throwing shoes in the Arab world at someone is considered to be contempt for an enemy. Many in the Middle East called the journalist heroic, but others thought the act was strictly unprofessional.

The TV networks in Iraq aired Bush ducking the shoes, and since he was not injured, the investigative judges may dismiss the case, or he could be charged with insulting a foreign leader and be sent to prison for two or three years. Many Iraqis' blame Bush for the murder of innocent Iraqi people.

Some Iraqis thought the act was the right time to express feelings about Bush and the war in Iraq. They felt it was time for someone to stand up to the American president. Authorities dismissed the sympathy act by some of the other journalist at the meeting. The Central Criminal Court of Iraq will make the decision on the charge of insulting a foreign leader. He could receive just a small fine.

Bush arrived back to the United States and kept his promise to bail out the auto companies. The billions in loans should help the staggering crisis, but it will force them to change how they operate.

Bush was criticized and accused of trying to protect his own legacy. Without help, the auto company crisis could flip the economy into a tailspin winding its way down a path of no return. The American auto companies have helped to build this economy into a super powerhouse.

The American people should ask themselves, "Is this the kind of people America should have in the Senate?" This is a Senate that voted themselves a pay raise at the taxpayer's expense.

The economy affects the whole world, yet conservation groups file lawsuits to block sale of oil-and-gas drilling leases. These people need to understand that American people do not like paying $4 gas hikes. America needs to adopt the slogan Drill Baby Drill that was heard so often during the campaign. Certain groups of people do not need to interfere with ongoing plans that will help the citizens of this country and the economy.

To top all other scandals in America's government, Illinois Gov. Rod Blagojevich was arrested on federal charges that he tried to sell President-elect Barack Obama's vacant Senate seat. He has ignored all calls to resign and denies all charges. This makes one wonder if the greed in the government will ever be dealt with.

Facts whether Barack's office had contact with the governor will be made available in due time according to a statement that Barack gave to the press.

Conversations by Chief of Staff Rahm Emanuel and Governor Blagojevich were found acceptable by Barack's transition team. The findings were appropriate, and the president-elect had no contact with Governor Blagojevich about filling his Senate seat. This was a corrupt plan that just happened to be caught before taking place in America's government. The corruptness in the government is springing forth since Barack has been elected for president.

Caroline Kennedy, daughter of the former president John F. Kennedy, wanted to replace Sen. Hillary Clinton in the Senate but dropped her name for reasons unknown. Some of the politicians complained about her inexperience. They thought that she had less than some of the other politicians seeking the Senate seat. A new senator cannot be appointed until Clinton is officially the secretary of state.

The year 2008 will end in a few days. The presidential election is the top story and the economic slump close behind. Oil prices soared. A gallon of regular gas peaked a little above $4.00 and fell below $1.70. The reason given on news stations was people were not driving as much.

Former Illinois Attorney General Roland Burris was appointed by Governor Blagojevich to take Barack's Senate seat. Burris was turned away at the Senate door and not allowed to take the appointed seat. Burris swiftly filed a lawsuit and was later sworn in to take the seat he felt entitled to.

Barack chose the Reverend Rick Warren to lead the inauguration prayer. Warren opposes abortion and same-sex marriage, an issue that causes division in many churches.

Gay-rights activists criticized Barack over picking Warren to give the invocation accusing him of believing with Warren's views on religion. The activists believe Warren's views are offensive and discriminatory.

Barack has said from the start he believes in a marriage between a man and a woman. He believes a woman should have a choice about abortion. He knows that not everyone agrees and believes alike, but we have to focus on things that are important. The problems America is experiencing is the most critical issue to be focused on at the present time.

A lawyer filed a petition claiming that Barack was born in Kenya. He wants Barack's Hawaiian birth certificate investigated to see if it is a valid document. The certificate states Barack was born in Hawaii on August 4, 1961. The lawsuit is just another attack for Barack to smile about and put behind him before becoming the most important person in the United States.

There is no way Barack can be or ever be a geek as some of his fans think. The standard he possesses is much too high, and his intellect goes way beyond a geek's intelligence. Barack is keen on technology and gets excited about future scientific viewpoints, giving him an advantage in the presidency. America should be proud to know that he is so well informed.

The plans that Barack has presented to America for the future can create new ways for technology to emerge, creating millions of jobs. This may well be the "American Dream" Barack talked about in his speeches so often on the campaign trail. Emerging technology brings an increase in research to advance ways in which engineers and scientists operate.

Barack loves technology and has appointed a chief technology officer, a person who sits in the room where decisions are made. This can be good news for technology and science to create different ways to use future technology.

America is so glad that Barack is able to ignore criticism. There is a great deal of jealousy and slander attacking him because he won the election—make no assumptions how he did it, just accept it.

Barack is very good at ignoring attacks and slander. Always with a big smile that sets him apart from other politicians, his attitude and smile was like a breath of fresh air coming out of Washington. There will probably be some news stations reporting that he smiles too much. Maybe he will take it as a compliment and keep on smiling.

Barack has taken a lot of slander mostly because there are people bent on destroying what he wants to do as president and because he is so popular with the people that voted for him. These kind of people should wise up and think about America and what they can do to help Barack turn a bad economy around.

PART 5

UPS AND DOWNS OF
THE TRANSITION

The new year 2009 begins with Southerners calling Barack a Yankee. They say he wants to destroy the South. Barack wants to destroy the ignorance in the South that still exists, not the South itself. Many Southerners did die in vain during the Civil War because of Yankees, but they died because they wanted free labor, refusing to set blacks free to live normal lives. Blacks were murdered, and many were raped at the hands of Southerners. They have fought a good fight to be accepted in what was a white world.

The New Mexico governor Bill Richardson withdrew as Barack's choice for commerce secretary. There is a grand jury investigation into his administration, and there are questions arising about his fundraising actions. Richardson's withdrawal was unpleasant, but unlike Governor Blagojevich, he acted with dignity.

Gov. Rod Blagojevich was impeached by a majority of votes in the Illinois House by lawmakers. He insisted that he didn't commit a crime and expressed that he himself was the victim in the ongoing case. He has not offered any explanation other than wanting to extend health care to ordinary people that are hurting in every state of America. He did not testify before the impeachment committee to argue his case on his criminal charges.

While the Senate and Congress argue over bailouts and who may be accepted to take Barack's Senate seat, the economy is still down, a war is raging between Palestinians and Israel, and the American people are "robbed" of their life savings that they invested with Bernard Madoff.

People should realize Israel is pounding Gaza with bombs to survive. The terrorist are sending rockets into their territory, and Israel is protecting themselves and their land. The peace that Israel seeks can only come by fighting back to regain their strength. They have the right to live in their land and protect it.

The destruction of Gaza may be the only hope Israel may have to survive such conflict.

Barack has been criticized by the Hamas leader for being silent. The group is a terrorist organization and a huge obstacle to "peace" in the Middle East. They oppose all talks with Israel and send a clear message of hate for the Jews. A portion of the land will not satisfy their hunger for a state.

The UN stopped aid to Gaza, and it may deepen the crisis. More than half of the territory's people live on food from the UN; and if hunger becomes a crisis to the people, an all-out war may erupt between Israel and Gaza, preventing a cease-fire.

Israel is not giving up and is attacking with full force. Gaza City is a fireball where thousands of Palestinians live south of Gaza City. Thick smoke is hanging, forming a huge black cloud over the area.

President Bush sweated out a question-and-answer session, giving his version of a sustainable cease-fire. He made it clear that Hamas needs to stop firing rockets into Israel. Bush is a strong president on foreign relations. He believes all countries have a right to protect their people and the land they live on.

Bush admitted making mistakes on the Iraq war, and not finding weapons of mass destruction was his biggest disappointment. His mistake of putting Mission Accomplished on an aircraft must have been very embarrassing to him and also the United States since it implied victory in Iraq, and the fighting got worse as terrorists came from other countries.

If Congress goes along with a request from Bush to give Barack the final bailout fund that Barack wants fast access to, he will have the opportunity to impose tougher restrictions on how the money is spent. The bailout fund that reaches in the millions should have a watchdog to oversee how it is spent.

Congress wants a health insurance program for children ready for Barack to ponder over when he takes office, a plan that he has requested and insisted on. He is aware of the growing need of a children's program in the United States to become law.

If Congress fails to supply a recovery plan, millions of jobs will be lost; and if the plan fails, the recession will deepen into a hole out of sight. The plan needs to create jobs that will give Americans back their life.

Barack wants to gain the people's trust and get credit flowing again through the banks to businesses and families. Once credit starts flowing, the recession should start lifting.

After weeks of criticism from gay-rights groups, Barack decided to select an openly gay bishop say a prayer at his inauguration. A move that does not in any way discredit his opinions about marriage or his beliefs. Barack has made it clear where he stands on the issue.

Bishop V. Gene Robinson believes Barack will support gay rights because he is black and understands discrimination, and maybe he does, but this is a discriminating world, and many people do not agree with gay rights nor do they want to try and understand why some persons are different. Should more evidence come to light supporting the fact of the matter to the cause or purpose creating such behavior, one may be inclined to believe in the gay-rights movement.

Sen. Hillary Clinton, secretary of state, chosen by Barack, is not wasting any time doing her job and was welcomed by the Senate Foreign Relations Committee. She was critical of the Bush administration's policy and the way they were treating the needs of the military.

Timothy Geithner, President-elect Barack's pick for the Treasury Department, owes back taxes; and he said he was not aware of the error. He committed to paying the taxes and the interest to the Internal Revenue Service. The officials decided the error was no big deal and proposed to drop the matter since it was not serious enough for him to be disqualified. Ordinary people do not understand how government can balk at paying their taxes for so many years and get away with it.

Senate Finance Committee Chairman Max Baucus decided a treasury secretary was needed in spite of these errors, believing they are serious, but should not prevent him from taking the office.

The Senate advanced legislation to set aside millions of acres as wilderness property not to be touched or explored. There were enough votes to overcome all the stalling that has taken place by the GOP, setting the plan in place to become law. If the law is passed, untouched property can be a vision of beauty.

Former President Bill Clinton's childhood home is being considered in a law that will designate it as a historic site. National parks, rivers, and other resources will be protected if the law passes.

Many analysts think the American auto companies are done. Chrysler in bad need, they say, cannot make it another year. They cannot turn the company around. The auto companies are what help drive the economy and should be helped as well as the banks.

U.S. sales of Chrysler, Dodge, and Jeep brand vehicles have fallen to an all-time low, the worst decline in the automaker's history. Workers' jobs and retirement are at stake. These good-paying jobs help support the economy.

President Bush gave a farewell address to the nation and admitted he made mistakes and tough decisions. His speech gave the impression he was trying to defend his actions. These actions brought heartache and confusion to people who had loved ones go to war.

President Bush is leaving with a high disapproval rating but a "thankful heart." He thanked America and often smiled during his speech. He seemed more than glad to pass the burdens of the world on to Barack, who thinks he has the answers to a failing economy going haywire.

Bush said he leaves with gratitude and is thankful for the trust the American people have given him. He will return home to his ranch and enjoy his retirement in Texas. His presidency, with all its problems, must have been a nightmare that was consistent.

Barack will be inaugurated as president of the United Stated in a few days and President Bush will be greeting the first black president. He thinks it is a great time in history that brings hope to all African Americans.

People are speculating what Barack will do as president. If there will really be a change and if the promises that brought so much support in the election will be implemented.

Barack has pledged a change and has power in some areas, but Washington sometimes is hardball and very stubborn to deal with. Some actions seem to never go anywhere since they have to travel so many paths to be recognized and voted on.

Barack as president will have the power in some areas of the government and can voice his opinions, but the public may have different opinions, and he may have to postpone his, resulting in the fact some may not get done at all.

Senate Democrats and Republicans were pleased with Barack's selected Cabinet positions giving him a plus in being able to choose wisely. The nation's economy is sending an urgent need to Barack and the officials.

The moment is nearing for Barack to take the oath of office and a passing of the torch is a term used often when a generation passes. He will be one of the youngest presidents to take office.

The baby boomer years are ending; and Barack, born in 1961, is a baby boomer that seeks to draw a line between himself and other politicians that came before him, setting him apart from the contrasting facts that are recorded in the nation's history.

People who know Barack say he is for real, not artificial. They don't believe politics will change him after he becomes president. He represents a new generation and has ideas he wants to communicate to the public. The torch has been passed to a new generation of Americans.

Barack wants everyone to get involved and express their ideas to him. This is a new kind of government that Americans are not used to but seem to be enjoying the challenge.

Will politics and the government become too big for Barack and stifle the smiles and outgoing personality he so well carries with him in public? We will see.

Years ago, African Americans were treated as if being black was a crime. Barack has said that he is proud of his heritage, and the world didn't give him a choice of what color he wanted to be. He is happy with who he is and what he looks like, so the rest of America should be.

There is not a white blood or a black blood as some people seem to think and try to whiten a person. All people have red blood, and color will not wash off. Black is beautiful. If it wasn't, people would not bake themselves in the sun.

Barack doesn't want to be white, and that should tell the civil rights movement to back away and stop their nonsense about his physical appearance. He thinks that he is black, and he is comfortable with it.

Barack was born in Honolulu and lived with his grandmother, who he dearly loved. She became ill during the campaign and did not get to enjoy seeing Barack elected as president. He visited her during her illness, and she died soon after.

Barack attended a Catholic school as a young child while living with his mother and stepdad but, at the age of ten, decided to live with his grandparents in Hawaii.

He was very active in sports and popular with all of the students. He left at the age of eighteen to enter college and decided what path he wanted to take as an adult. The years ahead would prove to be in his favor.

Barack pursued his education, earned his degrees, and decided to enter politics. He fought his way up in the world where success was just waiting for him to reach out and grab it.

The president-elect is an emotional kind of guy and choked up a bit when he left his home, but the airplane ride to Washington was a pleasant trip, and his mind returned to the problems facing him upon his arrival. Problems that he knew would not be easy to handle.

Atheists are at work once again in our government working their ugly deeds to try and have So Help Me God removed from the inauguration oath. This lawsuit should be thrown out and never allowed back in any court. Most Americans are religious people and have freedom of speech to acknowledge a "Great God" however and whenever the occasion justifies it. These people are trying to make their own laws and force them on every one else.

The U.S. Constitution is mostly about being faithful to the office of the president, protecting and defending America to the best of one's ability. Barack has promised to protect this country during the campaign.

So Help Me God does not have to be added, but Barack being a Christian most likely will add the words. He has the choice to express his faith. America was built on faith, and most people believe that there is a God. More than 85 percent claim some sort of religious belief.

Christians have the right to express their belief in God the way they choose, and no one should be able to disqualify it. One may wonder why so many people want to try and destroy what America stands far.

Barack, Joe, Jill, and Michelle took a four-day rail trip, the same path Lincoln took in the 1800s. The history was amazing across the miles. The scenery was a picture of beauty and looked as if it came out of a book. The four of them were astonished at the "risks" men took to declare America independent from Britain.

Barack was at ease throughout the journey and took in the history that the trip so well portrayed. The ratifying of the Constitution and the poem "The Star-Spangled Banner" were two important parts that inspired the four of them, and they could hardly wait to tell the stories to others.

Crowds appeared along the way wanting a peek at the president to be. Hundreds, who must have voted for Barack, wanted some kind of gesture from him to show that he appreciated all the votes from his supporters.

Barack decided to do charity work on the Martin Luther King Jr. holiday and put out the word for volunteers, thousands of people came to help with all the charity projects to honor King.

Barack and Vice President-elect Joe Biden made sure that the call included them. Barack must be good at painting. He rolled up his sleeves and painted at a homeless shelter while Biden hung dry wall at a Habitat for Humanity home.

Barack has a reputation of being a great political speaker, and his inauguration will be compared to Dr. Martin Luther King's "I have a dream" speech. King brought hope to blacks at a time in history when it was needed most.

Barack also has a reputation of being one of the best political speakers of our time. He must inspire and comfort a nation fighting two wars that has devastated an economy and people's lives.

Over several weeks, Barack worked carefully on his first speech to be presented as president. He wants his themes and his vision to be inspiring and made clear to the public.

Inauguration Day, Barack will take the Oath of Office using President Lincoln's Bible. After the inaugural address, he will escort President Bush to a ceremony and then attend a luncheon in his honor. This is a day that deserves celebrating, and there will be quite a bit going on before the day ends.

There will be ten inaugural balls for the new president and first lady to attend after the famous Inaugural Parade down Pennsylvania Avenue to the White House. They were often seen walking and waving to the people watching on each side.

<<<IMAGE>>>

Barack Obama chose Abraham Lincoln's Bible to lay his
hand on and be sworn in as President of the United States of
America. On March 4, 1861, Lincoln took the oath of office
and became the sixteenth President of the United States.
Lincoln was assassinated on the evening of April 14, 1865.
John Wilkes Booth shot the President in the head from the rear
of the presidential box.

PART 6

THE INAUGURATION

More than one million people were determined to see the inauguration of the first African American to become president of the United States. They gathered early under a bright January sky.

The swearing in of the new president was quite awkward to Barack since the opening words were stumbled over by Chief Justice John G. Roberts Jr., but Barack noticed the error and repeated the right words of the oath of office slightly out of order.

Barack closed with the words, "So help me God." Those words are not included in the constitutional oath but have become part of the presidential tradition. Some people believe they were added by President George Washington. Even though there is no proof of it, we know our forefathers built America on faith in God.

President Barack said in his inaugural address:

> The challenges we face are real, they are serious, and they are many. They will not be met easily or in a short span of time. But know this, America—they will be met.
>
> We have gathered here because we have chosen hope over fear, unity of purpose over conflict and discord. To end petty grievances and false promises.
>
> We remain a young nation, but in the words of Scripture, the time has come to reaffirm our enduring spirit; to choose our better history; to carry forward that precious gift, that noble idea, passed on from generation to generation: the God-given

promise that all are equal, all are free and all deserve a chance to pursue their full measure of happiness.

Let it be said by our children's children that when we were tested we refused to let this journey end, that we did not turn back nor did we falter; and with eyes fixed on the horizon and God's grace upon us, we carried forth that great gift of freedom and delivered it safely to future generations.

During the inaugural address, Barack asked Americans to sacrifice for America's sake. He knows most people already are, and many have lost their incomes, preventing a way to pay their bills.

Most Americans believe this country is willing to help Barack get the economy moving in an upward position. They see a tough road ahead for him and can predict the next four years will be bumpy.

This new president has a load of promises to carry during his time in office. It won't be easy for him to live up to all the plans, but his victory will embrace the fact it is a time in history to succeed. Many blacks thought his victory would not happen in their lifetime, and they were overjoyed to see him win.

The change he hopes will materialize requires supporters and opponents working together and accepting each other's opinions, a theory that will be extremely difficult for some to accept.

Barack and the first lady were all smiles as they walked down Pennsylvania Avenue during the inaugural parade. Michelle's yellow sheath dress sparkled in the sun. President Barack's red tie and white shirt peaked out from his suit that was topped with an overcoat bearing an American flag pin. They waved at the people standing on the sides of the street.

Their daughters, ten-year-old Malia and seven-year-old Sasha, were also in style for the occasion. A double-breasted periwinkle blue coat with a blue ribbon bow at the waist set Malia off from her sister, who wore a pink coat with an orange scarf and satin belt.

Meanwhile the world celebrates Barack taking office. It triggered joy in a world weary of war and a recession. Bulls and goats were slaughtered for feasts in Kenya. There were toasts at black-tie balls in Europe indicating hope for better days ahead.

Children watched the swearing in of Barack on TV, and they bowed their heads in prayer as Pastor Rick Warren gave the invocation. Children recognize the need to pray for Barack and the economy as the need becomes stronger.

A letter sent to Barack from Nelson Mandela, the former South African president, stated that Barack's election to a high office inspired people all over the world and brought hope of change to a dying economy. Barack's voice was heard loud and clear by many hoping for a better world.

Students from Barack's former school in Indonesia wore traditional costumes and celebrated his election. The tropical islands are known for their bright costumes and celebrations.

Rully Dasaad, a former classmate of Barack, was proud that he knew the president and had shared time with him as children. They learned tolerance, how to share and to accept differences in cultures and religions. One could guess this school is where Barack learned how to be a leader.

Barack has the country more united than any other president has been able to do, yet some people do not agree with his policies, and it causes unity to be fragile. The reality of certain events can become a matter of concern.

Some people think that there is not a man that can live up to the huge support Barack has managed to accumulate. He will often be forced to make tough decisions but will suddenly realize they cannot be implemented. He has a goal in mind, but it may have to be put on hold for a while.

Every president has left office with a lower approval rating than when he entered office, excluding Bill Clinton. Barack's approval ratings are "higher" than any president in the past. The public's favor for the new president is astounding.

Mistakes will more than likely be made, and there will be some success in many plans. We have to expect some disappointment; no one is "perfect." The first two years will be critical, mainly because of the economy and the wars.

While Barack celebrates his inauguration, his Guantanamo order could come as soon as this very week. Closing the Cuba detention camp is the first step toward restoring order to the terror fight. Barack will put much attention to the economy and also keeping the nation safe.

Secret Service officials were appointed to the presidential inauguration after news of a possible attack by Somalia-based militants. The threat did not specify Washington DC and came from an individual overseas. The attack did not take place as predicted and could have been a scare tactic to try and postpone the inauguration. The president and first lady felt safe with all the security surrounding them on all sides. It was the largest security operation ever to be appointed to a presidential inauguration.

PART 7

THE PRESIDENCY

God wants rulers in power to govern fairly and always with justice. He can use humans, whether their intentions are good or evil, to accomplish his purpose, which is always good.

America has high expectations for President Barack Obama—maybe too high, but the public has taken the young family to heart as they move into the White House. They have been shown much appreciation and respect.

Barack intends to lead with strength. He clearly understands the problems confronting him and the nation; he is so ready to work on them. He provides the nation with an opportunity to move forward together. He calls for an end to "putting off unpleasant decisions." He is calling for a new way of thinking and to adopt an entirely new perspective.

Barack's first day in office finds him signing an executive order to close the prison at Guantanamo Bay. He ordered major changes that would halt the torture of suspects, ban secret CIA prisons oversees, and fight terrorism in a manner that is consistent with our values and our ideals.

Barack has only been in office a few days and is getting criticized for supporting abortion and closing Guantanamo Bay. Criticism is to be expected since he is not perfect; and many people do not share the same beliefs, thoughts, or plans.

Barack is "idealistic" and acts according to his high ideals, regardless of circumstances. He believes America is above torture, and so we should be. If our actions are according to terrorists' actions, are we any better than they are? Torture and violence can only breed hate into hearts that do not know God.

If you consider someone an enemy, you should give him food to eat and, if thirsty, give him water to drink. In doing this, you will heap burning coals on his head, and the Lord will reward you. Sometimes good deeds and not revenge will prick an enemy's conscience.

Barack believes a woman should have the right to have an abortion but also that there should be programs teaching about prevention. In many cases, if there is not a legal abortion clinic, a woman may seek out someone not qualified, and it results in death. Not everyone believes life starts at conception and will determine to have abortions and commit murder regardless of God's laws or the government's laws.

Congress has decided to give Barack $825 billion to help the economy and create jobs. The president already has $350 billion for banks to extend loans to small businesses.

The $700 billion Barack won permission to spend will help to weatherize some people's homes giving them relief from winter's cold. It will boost spending for various projects such as new buses.

The deficit is in the trillions, and people are saying the government is overspending. The economy may never recover from a debt so huge. Trillions is hard to comprehend for most Americans that live on so little and cannot see their way out of all the debts making their lives unbearable.

Critics are saying the plan may not work and America may need a larger stimulus plan that will cost taxpayers even more in the future. The overspending is a risk to the economy, and critics are demanding answers to how such a plan this huge can possibly help an economy already in trouble.

Barack's presidency faces the highest deficit America has seen since a disastrous World War II, but he is not backing down and remains calm and willing to lead this country back to prosperity. His hopes may be out of sight and may frustrate some close-minded people. But hope is surely better than being pessimistic.

President Barack was right when he said, we all need to pitch in and do our part in this current crisis. Above all, the private sector and government regulators need to act responsibly.

Barack's inaugural address reminded America that if we are not watching, the market can spin out of control. If a nation favors the prosperous, the poor and middle class will suffer in all areas of their life. The market cannot be left to prosper only the one's that benefit from the global economy.

The president's recovery plan is needed to jump-start the sliding economy running away with millions of jobs, and millions more could be lost before any signs pointing to a turn around in the future. College dreams have become a nightmare instead of an "American Dream."

Important priorities concerning energy and education are an important part of Barack's program. Health care and new infrastructure are also necessary to be competitive in this uncertain economy. The future depends on strength in America's government.

Some people seem to think Barack is making a mistake, spending billions of dollars America doesn't have. If he is, we will find out in the near future. These tax cuts are not enough to supply the needs of some people that need much more.

The tax cuts would give $500 a year to individuals and $1,000 for couples. Employers would reduce the amount of tax withheld from employees' paychecks. Some people say the tax cuts are more of the same, and it is not change.

Even if the stimulus plan passes, it won't be a quick fix like some would presume. The economy with all its downturns will likely get worse. The recovery may be long and drawn out. Though painful as it sounds, it took eight years to get America in this major and unpleasant predicament; it may take eight more to find an outlet.

Timothy Geithner, sworn in as treasury secretary, will recommend and decide if more money will be needed for the banks, which are still not meeting demands to get the economy stable and moving upward to meet specifications.

Consumers continue to put off getting loans and buying new things. Loans cannot be approved unless a person has a job, and a person cannot buy if there are no jobs available.

Barack's plan will help senior citizens, giving them a bonus of $300. Seniors need a boost because most of them live on their social security check and cannot meet their bills.

His plan is designed to help the poor and disabled school children across the United States. Schools in every state are in need of government help. The no Child Left Behind fund needs the money to survive.

Barack has not agreed to any changes to his stimulus plan, but some Republicans want certain changes concerning tax relief for businesses to accommodate their needs.

There is little GOP support for Barack's plan, but he hopes that some of the lawmakers will support his ideas and vote for it. Republicans want a plan that will total 40 percent tax cuts.

As it turns out, not one Republican voted for Barack's plan, and some Democrats voted against it. Tax cuts are great, but what good are they if Americans do not have jobs. It is time for Republicans and Democrats to come together and think about the thousands of taxpayers that have had to put their lives on hold, just to survive this economic disaster.

The House approved an $800 billion stimulus plan at the taxpayers' expense, and the Senate is drawing up a plan of their own. Hopefully, they will come together for the benefit of taxpayers.

While they argue over what is best for everyone, there are enormous problems in our economy, and we the taxpayers have to help the financial problems that have become enormous because of overspending in our government.

Wall Street got a hot scolding from Barack for paying employees billions in bonuses last year while their financial system received a bailout from taxpayers.

It is "shameful" to think America's government has not provided for the American people's needs the way they should. There has been too much wasteful spending and has caused heartache for the rich and the poor.

We Americans should learn from our mistakes and know that wrong decisions will bring failure. We need to take care of our homeland and stop supporting countries that hate our very existence.

Barack is now in control of the wars in Iraq and Afghanistan, but he has not decided to bring the combat forces home as he planned to do during the campaign.

Peace in the Middle East would be a plus for our new president; many have tried and failed. Barack told the Muslim world that the United States is not their enemy, but can they really understand such a statement? Most of them have a polluted conscience and are rooted in customs or culture.

Barack thinks it is time for Israel to live in peace and promised to "seek" Middle East talks with Arab neighbors and Iran. Conflict has taken a toll on Israel, and it is time for peace to prevail.

Hillary Clinton, secretary of state, took her first trip overseas and warned North Korea that their possible missile launch would not help in relations with the United States. She delivered a strong message that

Barack and the United States are committed to a foreign policy that values what others have to say. She told them we will have differences, but we will discuss them and cooperate.

There are Jew haters in the world that would like to see Israel as a nation disappear. They also say the Holocaust didn't happen. These people are not only the enemy of Jews but America that supports Israel and recognizes they deserve peace.

Iran has caused unease among world leaders that are concerned about their missile programs. The claim of successfully launching a satellite is a death threat to the Middle East.

Ahmadinejad made a speech during the celebration of the country's thirtieth anniversary and said the country is ready for talks with the United States. America should take this remark with caution.

In order to stabilize the war in Afghanistan, the White House is adding seventeen thousand troops this year. It is necessary to seek out the terrorists and find their hiding places. The caves are a safe haven and hard to find.

Many people, because of the woes of the economy, have hit bottom and feel abandoned. They have lost their jobs and their homes. Barack understands their suffering, and he is trying to keep his promises. Severe and sudden calamity can destruct one's interests or prospects.

The economy has staggered even further into a tailspin. Shoppers are not buying anything, and the recession could last beyond what was expected. It could last for years. It seems to sink further into a pit of no return.

New orders by Barack will reverse the Bush administration's policy that favored employers over workers. This was needful to level the field for workers and unions. It should strengthen the labor movement.

Barack also signed a bill giving workers more time to sue for wage discrimination. Women over the years have worked for less pay than men yet doing the exact same work.

Because of greenhouse gas auto emissions, Barack wants better standards and the automakers to produce fuel-efficient cars. The auto industry expressed concern because of state and federal rules.

Researchers say the damage to the climate is basically irreversible. They say temperatures will remain high for several years. The temperature and changes in rainfall has been observed in many areas.

This is a nation that has been prosperous but has "polluted" the earth with all the technology invented over the years. There may be a methodical system to solve this problem; America just has to find it.

God provided many good gifts for America, and these gifts are not to be taken lightly, to rest on light-minded leaders who have thought only about wealth.

The beauty and order of the world is obviously the work of a skilled architect who carefully shaped the plans for a splendid structure. A wonderful masterpiece that only the artist can really appreciate.

There are people hoping President Barack fails in his plans for America. If he should fail, that would bring doom to America for sure. They think he wants a socialist America.

Socialism is the theory or system of social organization by which the means of production and distribution are owned, managed, or controlled by the government.

Barack's message to America has never suggested, by any means, that he "favors and supports" socialism. He has been very open about bringing people together in unity.

The president has set up an Internet Web site, white-house.gov, which will be overseen by Barack's director of new media. President Barack knows firsthand what people can do when they come together to get an accomplishment. He wants citizen participation, and the Web site is an important tool to include the public before signing important laws.

Barack knows technology can make American lives easier, and it is important to those who feel technology improves their life. Having someone in the White House who understands technology is good for everyone.

Perhaps no one knows how to get out of the current mess America is in. There is one fact for sure, Barack, unlike the Republicans, is trying to extend a hand out to them and repair the damage done over the years.

Barack has finally proven to America that he is not "messianic." He did what most presidents will not do. In making a statement, he made a mistake. Human he is, and he takes responsibility for his mistakes

Tom Daschle withdrew his nomination to become secretary of health and human services because of unpaid taxes. This was a blow to Barack since Daschle was to have led the efforts to make "affordable" health care coverage available to all Americans.

Nancy Killefer withdrew as chief performance officer. Now we may ask ourselves, "How in the world did these leaders in our government get away with tax transgressions?" Ordinary Americans have to pay taxes out of hard-earned salaries, often living from paycheck to the next paycheck, while leaders in power make excuses. They "forgot" about a law that is forced upon us to pay for education, roads, etc.

Not only are leaders backing out on Barack, negotiations have not gone well between Republicans and Democrats on the stimulus bill. Republicans want the same old policy of tax cuts.

The differences between these two political parties are frustrating without "normal action" and therefore unable to function in detail. Action is an important step in solving a crisis such as this one.

If Republicans keep holding back, delaying what Barack is trying to do for the American people, he may well have to shut out the party even though he very much wants to unite and be at peace.

News of a big loss of jobs brought forward a deal that is expected to move the stimulus plan through the Senate. Democratic leaders believe they have enough support to pass the legislation.

Not many Republicans signed the agreement, forcing Barack to take his campaign on the road. These Republican lawmakers are determined to see our new president fail, thus bringing disappointment to the American people.

Barack, already missing his freedom, needed to get away from the White House and the media. He left Washington to try and sell his economic plan among the people that needs help from it.

He will celebrate Lincoln's two hundredth birthday in Illinois. Presidents of both parties have honored Lincoln, and two hundred years after his birth, they still want to honor him in words as well as action. Present Barack compares himself to Lincoln and announced his candidacy on Lincoln's birthday. During the celebration the president and first lady were presented with a copy of Lincoln's Gettysburg Address.

February is celebrated as Black History Month, a time when America recognizes and celebrates the progress our black citizens have made in our nation. Giving blacks a short month of commemoration seems to set apart black from white, not that America doesn't want to acknowledge the importance of black citizens. It just seems it should be all year.

There is still much discrimination in America, mostly in the South, where many educated adults lack perspective about the Civil War. America can and must do more to end discrimination. It is an injustice to the black race and not fair; justice is meant to be for all people.

Even in our court systems, where crimes are punished years after they are committed, justice prevails.

The very sad news is many American soldiers are committing suicide and will be a reminder to their families and friends of a war that maybe should not have been. The damaged minds and bodies created scars so deep the nightmares may never cease.

It has been eight years of turmoil in a strange and war-torn country, and the U.S. military is stretched and strained from a long and persistent warfront.

Barack may disappoint Americans and back off withdrawing troops in sixteen months, which is not good news; but if it helps keep America safe, we should not complain.

Disappointment over Middle Eastern oil is another fact to consider. Americans cannot afford the high price of gas, and the oil-rich countries control the output. They seem to enjoy having some power over the United States, to complicate the way we live.

The Republicans continue to disappoint not only Barack but Americans in withdrawing from their nominations. Judd Gregg of New Hampshire withdrew his position as commerce secretary.

Only three Republicans voted for Barack's economic stimulus plan, but Barack thinks it is important to build bipartisan consensus around important issues, such as the $787 billion stimulus bill that passed through Congress. It gave Barack a victory and now will go to his desk to sign.

Since Barack took office on January 20, he has signed legislation extending government-financed health care to millions of lower-income children. He has also signed a job discrimination order for workers to sue their employers.

No one knows if this stimulus agreement will create jobs or just be about spending. Barack thinks jobs; Republicans think it is all about spending, and it may take years to find out the answer.

Barack admitted the plan is not perfect, but no one knows a better way to fix the mess America is confronting. Barack wants to keep his promises, and he is being honest. He is doing something to combat doing nothing.

The stimulus plan contains help on taxes that will give workers $13 extra in their weekly paychecks. A $1,000 child tax credit for low-income families. It will help many workers who lose their health insurance, help millions who live in poverty.

This economic crisis is hurting the very rich as well as the very poor. Being too rich is often thought of as being greedy. This crisis has manifested itself into household incomes that ordinarily enjoy the "finer" possessions in life.

There are many questions to be asked, and there are many people asking, but no one is giving out answers. The answer may well lie in our own destructive habits. America has thrived and taken advantage of wealth, often ignoring signs that trouble quietly sleeps on the surface of the cornerstone.

Much is to be done and not enough time to get this crisis under control. We need to support our new president and give him the space he needs instead of all the criticism. Faultfinding brings no fair treatment where deserved.

The muddy water is deep, strong, and dark with extreme deeper parts. The water must be purified to remove all the "corruptness" America has seen the past few years.

This once prosperous nation will not prosper again until the cesspool is completely cleaned of all the rubbish, meeting the requirements to see clearly.

If America thinks Barack is wrong in what he states about tax cuts, one should ask themselves why Bush's tax cuts didn't work.

Bush's stimulus plan sold America out to the Chinese, billions we the taxpayers will have to pay back. Our children and grandchildren will pay back through the nose. Where did the money go, and did it help the economy now drowning in debt? No, it did nothing for America but put a few dollars in the richest hand's pocket.

The bottom line is people are scared and they are not spending money; therefore, the economy is sinking. People are losing their nest eggs in the market and through shady dealings.

Jobs are being cut in the auto industry, which needs billions more to stay afloat. Delphi is cutting 800 jobs, and our manufacturing jobs continue to vanish in all states. The United States still is the world's leading manufacturer. This could change if our government doesn't handle this crisis in a productive manner.

Some states' congressmen say the stimulus is not practical or not well thought out. Everyone has the right to their own opinion; however, we have got to give it a chance.

The negative attacks are still popping up here and there, but why should Barack care, after all he is the most powerful person in the United States; and one thing is for sure, he doesn't give up.

The latest attack appears to compare Barack to a chimpanzee, and civil rights leaders are saying it is racist. The writer apologized and said the cartoon refers to the stimulus bill as being badly written.

The attack over the Health Care Reform, claims President Barack wants to exterminate unhealthy persons, forces doctors to give up their independence in practicing medicine.

You can form your own opinion; however, couldn't it be that the government wants to put a stop to unneeded tests and hospital stays that is costing millions and robbing social security?

There is criticism over the housing plan to halt mortgage foreclosures. We all are going to pay in the end to get this economy moving back to normal, if not it will deepen. Barack is trying to stabilize the housing market, and Americans are watching this plan as it moves in the direction of the projects it is intended for.

We should be thankful Barack rejects rejection and considers the fact that all the apples in a basket are not rotten. He has the power and skill to laugh at unnecessary feelings. His audacious spirit always arouses one's interest and overtakes annoying criticisms.

Yes, our life as Americans has turned upside down, a price we must pay for all the lavish spending of two wars—the rich getting richer off the less fortunate so they can feed their appetites. The greedy always want more than their share. They have a hungry desire to possess more than what is reasonable.

Barack took a trip to Canada to offer assurances of his support for cross-border commerce. Canada is the largest trading partner of the United States, and Barack wants a greater trade agreement. Canada, being a longtime friend of the United States, our president doesn't want to take them for granted.

It was a seven-hour visit among the Canadians, who admire Barack and celebrated his arrival with a fried-dough pastry called beaver tail—the icing formed a huge O to represent Obama.

It would be pleasing if all Americans were refined and thoughtful enough to consider other's feelings and stop discriminating "remarks" and "stories" that only help to fan the flame burning out of control.

Maybe someday, we can all look back, hopefully, not too far in the future and see just how ridiculous all these blame games are.

Barack is using all the weapons he has against the bombastic words. Words that cut to the bone and heart of a leader trying to bring America together to solve a deadly crisis. America must stop the nonsense and help our elected leader. If not, we may face a homeless catastrophe that brings ruin to many people.

Food could be scarce and money hard to come by. Only the persons who have land to grow their grain and meat will survive. Money is disappearing as the economy weakens.

Retirement plans are being put on hold as Americans calculate just what to do in a failing economy they once believed in and trusted.

The "panic button" can be turned off, and the unreasoning fear that has spread through a multitude of people is capable of being restrained.

People sometimes believe that which is worse through unreliable sources. One should reason out what is said and think through one's own opinion before acting.

For the sake of America and the American people, we can have loving-kindness and respect for one another, a "reverent devotion" to our country and our president.

Barack knows he is not God and does not pretend that he is a "Supreme Being." He doesn't have a divine nature. He is loved because of who he is, his ideas, and believing that he can make a difference. The effect and influence he has on certain people is differential and unusual.

The love affair is not about Barack; it is about hope, the expectation that centers in what he desires for all Americans. This affair or business matter concerns the least to the greatest, the poor and the famous.

Without hope there is not a reason to succeed in a bad or disagreeable condition. Hope will make one's heart sing and count their blessings one by one. A wish for happiness or success makes one happy and contented.

Barack has hope that he can cut the federal deficit in half in four years. For the economy to grow, the deficit has to shrink. Former President Clinton was able to shrink a growing deficit and that promotes hope for President Barack's plan.

Barack wants to cut back on Iraq war spending and raise taxes on the wealthiest taxpayers to help reduce the deficit. It is a part of his campaign speeches that helped to get him elected.

Some Republican governors refuse the help the stimulus bill would give to help their states. This rejection could hurt many people that are out of work while the governors themselves are quite comfortable.

All the negative talk about the economy only adds fuel to a fire already burning out of control. There may not be a master plan to die down the flames and eventually douse the hot coals, but we need to stand by our president and respect what he is trying to do for America.

It is hard for some pessimistic thinkers to think about a recovery when obviously they have not hit the bottom of the bucket. Once you hit the bottom, you can see all the dirt.

Dirt can accumulate anywhere. Even in government, people that are supposed to help in any way possible to aid our ailing country sometimes forget what is really important in solving problems.

People that are against Barack and his plans to turn this economy into a positive direction are against the economy itself, resulting in doom and gloom for all taxpayers.

America needs positive thinkers, people with an open mind that can see and feel the painful suffering that is unpleasant and surmounting causing depression and sadness.

All the gloomy forecasters need "faith" that can move mountains and rise to a higher level of action to be able to deal with the high ground to advance this nation toward a rebound.

Faith is trusting and being worthy of trust. Fraud and deception has no reasonable ground or occasion to be in America's ruling and control over this country.

This land has to countermarch and be counteroffensive to stop the wild ideas that run counter to common sense and defeat the plot that has "cunningly and secretly" made an entrance into our government.

These wild ideas can defeat the very purpose that a country needs to prosper and be in control to form a healthful economy that provides the necessary conditions that worthy Americans need to survive.

PART 8

THE THEORY

The formation of ideas can form a plan or belief in the mind that fancies a perfect theory that everyone approves of. This can complicate any explanation based on thought.

All the elected officials want a finger in the pie and twist the facts out of proportion. The finger-pointing is thoughtless and will fail to be positive in consideration of others.

Confusion only makes affairs worse. It causes fear, and the complexity only puzzles everyone involved. America wants answers to why their government cannot and will not work together on this hard task.

America's government makes thin excuses, has scanty relationships from one side to the other side. The depth of reasoning is third-rate and somewhat touchy. This touch and go bubble may burst and needs to be treated lightly.

Barack is cooperating with the other officials and welcomes their input on all matters that he has suggested; however, none of them has come up with a better scheme for a plan.

America's failing market is in a psychotic state and needs definite psychotherapy. This is a critical moment that requires analysis to examine all features to explain such a downcast.

A new diagram could be tricky and send a false message that it is not real, that it is a clever act to play tricks on an unsuspecting nation. The drawing should show the important parts and clearly explain how it works.

A workable plan should persuade or influence the method into a work of art. This workmanship will show how worldly-wise America can be.

Having or showing knowledge and good judgment allows one to give wise information and instruct a particular or definite condition indicating a purpose.

The aim or intention made should purr with good results and pursue a wise course that takes no chances. It is an opportunity to be optimistic about particular circumstances that coexist.

Under no circumstances should minor details be compared with main facts. Main facts give full and exact details that support or prove a factor.

A factor has to be established as true, made certain, and be found to be genuine. It has to be subject to some testing process, and in time the course will be finished. The trial will give evidence and bear witness to the substance used in the examination.

Substance is the main body in a rumor or a claim, and the matter will give concrete form to a theory. Many forms have little or no real meaning, just blank spaces to be filled in. A form has to be composed and developed to a gradual unfolding to be worked out in detail.

Sometime in the future, maybe the U.S. government will put across the purpose and proceed to take advantage of putting an end to a perplex problem.

The problematic cure for the economy has caused Americans to be "doubtful and uncertain" about everything America stands far. America's position and reputation is in danger.

Americans need a good standard of living that will provide comfort, happiness, upright support to depend on and rise to their feet to take a stand against an enemy that "refuses" to yield.

This energetic and active force has "strength and power" that drains the very quality of life Americans depend on, making it necessary to have a life preserver.

Americans saw Barack as their lifesaver, to save them from drowning in the "murky and gloomy" darkness cutting off the air they breathe. Barack provided the air hole. He became the needed aid and had an air of hope.

The hopeless feeling became an expectation, and he was the center of it. He gave people a reason to hope against hope. Where there is hope, there is trust to rely on. Barack is America's trustee. He is responsible for the affairs of the United States. People saw him as a trusty leader.

Barack gave guidance and direction in his campaign speeches and answered questions so worded that it suggested the answer desired. People wished strongly for a better plan or system, and he gave it to them.

The infectious disease attacking America's government and economy is symptomatic of political unrest. There is a disturbed condition that is unseemly and unhealthy.

America's economy must be brought back to a healthy condition and get a solution to the heartrending, heart-stricken problem that "crushes" the innermost heart with grief.

Barack delivered his first speech to Congress. Each part of his theory was in place and exactly what he promised the American people on the campaign trail. His speech was well-written and well-spoken.

This speech brought back the hope almost lost since the election. Barack's poll numbers are still high, but the economy is still in deep mud, so boggled down that it may take billions more to clear the clouded condition.

Once the promises start to be seen and recognized, the fear will disappear. Americans will be able to see clearly and begin to understand that the requirements are being met.

The economy is in constant requisition for a needed rebound to health. The restoration to a good condition will bring a favorable recognition and appreciation from the public.

The public as a whole deserve the service of every public manner to be open and showing an "unselfish desire" for the public good, making it helpful and useful.

An infected economy is overcome with gloomy forecasts and needs a new direction to settle all the dizziness of a "nervous shock." The violent shake can cause a sudden attack taking away the power to move. The intense jolt is painful and may need surgery to remove certain methods.

The powerhouse America once had needs a high-powered microscope to see all the small details holding back the detection of destructive methods. A microscopic eye can investigate all the mistakes of a failed process and change the condition.

A public official announcement of a cure from America's new president will give him a favorable advantage. It will mean points scored and mark a new beginning that is suitable and proper.

The official system should have excessive attention and an official routine. The routine methods need routine workers to sit at a round table, make round trips and round up every origin of germ cells that germinate and make them void.

This group of persons needs to be united for the same purpose and have original ability, fresh thinking and arise to a creative mind, being aware of all the creepers that creep slowly toward their victims and swindle the support of lividity. They need to bring back the full energy and activity of a present motionless livelihood that is needing an electric current to carry out one's ideas.

This theory should identify a set of doctrines theorizing unpractical opinions. Speculation is useless and is wasted time. It has no foundation and will not idle fears.

America has no faultless theory to present to an injured economy, but the injury can be healed, and the heartbeat of the American people can again be heartfelt with encouragement.

Barack has promised a new vision for America, a blueprint or copy of plans for a nation in a severe crisis. His budget blueprint will contain a variety of firmly formed, stern choices; but it is not a finished blueprint.

Barack's theory is being criticized, mostly by Republicans, but he is ambitious and determined to rescue this shaky and staggering economy proving to all the doubters that a challenge is a call to fight and demands victory.

There is a vicious enemy with wicked habits surrounding undesirable circumstances. Barack's hope is that the facts will sustain his theory and extend around all views.

Those views should be cleared from suspicion and defend successfully against opposition. The struggle against a different direction is contrary to action, resisting the advancement of openness.

Open-minded persons show a mind open to new ideas, and they settle undecided questions, making the passage clear and exposed to a general view of knowledge. True information is acquainted with experience.

Barack's theory is experimental, and cures are often found by experimenting with tests or trials to find out the cause of a complication that is hard to understand or settle.

To settle a claim, one must determine the arrangement of the position or way of life and settle upon an act of order that establishes a fixed course resulting in a settlement of balance with purpose.

Calling Barack names only brings uneasiness and anxiety to an upset market on the verge of a drastic downhill. The fall could be a heavy drop and overthrow some good ideas.

A disrespect for an elected official is disruptive and causes discontentment with a disconnection to freedom of choice to use wise caution. It destroys trust in the good name that stands in doubt.

A dispute breaks off friendly relations. Some quarrelsome people find it hard to accept change or a man of "color" in charge of U.S. problems. The change is to help persons not able to help themselves because of a failed economy and consumption of wealth by greedy leaders in management.

Barack's theory is a down payment on a debt to be paid by wealthy taxpayers, giving the middle class and the poor a chance for a quality way of living and not just an existence. The source of activity will influence society.

The common interest of society should be joined for a common purpose in community life that deals with all the facts and reasons of why a problem exists. If the problem is doubtful and uncertain, it becomes questionable.

A solution to a questionable problem may require a changing of the way a nation operates to produce a desired effect. It may need some addition or some subtraction to manage the operative measures. Using the right instruments can improve the health of a nation and make it whole, complete in itself.

America doesn't need all the mix-up or confused state of affairs that are hard to understand. The power of understanding is the ability to get the meaning of a comprehensive review.

The competition in America is so great that there is an effort to obtain self-satisfaction and complain about complex instructions for rebuilding America's government.

This process of drawing conclusions from facts leaves no room for restoration of courage and confidence to reassure a calmness in the recession that is moving backward.

By reclaiming independence, America will demand the return of a separate, distinct, independent manner that cannot be described or destroyed.

The anger concerning Barack's theory is unjust and mixed with scorn. It is an insult and lack of good judgment. The criticism is a misfortune enforced by bias opinions.

Opinions that are in a bewildered condition and complete confusion are under a spell that is beyond being broken. The opinions are weak and unfit for use in government.

With all the unfavorable talk, there is uneven ground to level before a foundation can be accurately laid. The unfounded complaints are baseless and ungrounded. They have no cause to draw conclusions without reasonable limits.

The senseless talk lessens a person's sensibilities to feel or perceive. There is a tendency to feel hurt or offended too easily. When one is offended, one is easily influenced.

Barack is a sensational speaker. He aroused strong and excited feelings in American people who had not had those sensations for a very long time. He made reasonable awareness of the problems America faces and gave impressions of having good judgment.

Barack's actions are influenced by his intellect and feelings. He faces problems in an intellectual way and is capable of being understood. He is direct in his speech having a purpose and intent to strengthen.

The design of his plan is deep and thorough giving emphasis on expressing action to connect the dots. He wants action in joining together with connected ideas that need to be put in proper order. Connected ideas will support bonded relations.

The plan Barack has presented to the American people is in relation to the future. Even though some people have rejected his plan and wants it to fail, he has absolute faith it will work.

Fighting against opposed persons is nothing new in Barack's life. There has been war and conflict throughout his successful life. He has the will and the desire to keep his campaign promises.

Promises that won him a great privilege and favor with the American people. The force coming against these promises is a violent strain on what America needs at the present time.

Pessimism has a tendency to look on the dark side and see difficulties plus disadvantages. This gloomy view of things only causes trouble and is annoying.

This disturbance makes people angry with America's government officials. They want a peaceful solution, they cringe at all the wishy-washy inferior knowledge and advice Washington hands out.

Barack is our advocate; and he speaks in our favor, pleads our defense, and argues for the plan we supported. He recommends publicly what he thinks is best for America in a high degree.

These beastly and brutal attacks are meant to stir up and rouse an anger most people are not accustomed to. These unwholesome attacks are not worthy and are shameful. They are not based on truth and are unwelcome to a nation wanting a stable economy.

This unsteady economy needs to be unshackled and set free of all the ugly, unpleasant snarls of unsociable behavior. The tiring tangles have got to be straightened to remove the confusion.

Confusion only bewilders many people causing blunders that embarrass a government already being judged severely. The harshness is sharp and very plain; the severity can cause a storm to move rapidly.

The violent outbreak can cause an outburst of angry words that produce heavy hail and blowing rain. This rainstorm can drench the sounds that have meaning, sending a signal of unexpressed spoken words. Meaningless words do not make sense and are not significant.

Measured words are "uniform" and have a capacity of dimensions. They have a standard of comparison, estimation, and judgment. They can judge one's character, moral strength, or weakness.

Words can distinguish one person from another person. Cheerfulness is a characteristic that we admire in people. Noticeable characteristics have special "qualities or features." Honesty attracts attention and gives a person a good reputation.

Barack attracted attention because he is different, has a big smile, is intellectual, is an inspiring speaker, and gives powerful speeches that show strength.

Barack has the power to control, influence, persuade, and convince groups of people wanting to act together. He can compel with unusual effort in a convincing, forcible speech. He has careful thoughts for the future.

This future includes our children and grandchildren. Yes, they will inherit our debt just as we all inherited the debt from our ancestors. They will also inherit a divided government that refuses to work together for the good of a great nation.

America cannot survive or stand in a divided working field. The disagreements separate the regions into different parts. Each section has too much artillery, and the commands are criticized.

The commander in charge has a theory how to win the war, but part of the army will not follow his instructions. There is no commitment to his authority or the direction that leads to victory.

The command gives the information about where to go, what to do, points to the aim of the directions, and is straightforward. There are no bends or curves. It is a straight course, making every move free from pain or trouble.

A remarkable turnaround depends on the theory of a leader. The leader must have wisdom and a wise plan to be carried out. A follower is one who follows the ideas or beliefs of the leader. They follow through together to the end, and the result is hard to tell until the conclusion.

A good leader has a clear awareness of the dangers they must face and are prepared to use action at once. He restores encouragement to those who have lost hope or meaning in their life.

Part of the battle is mental activity, making decisions, presenting a speech, pressure to deliver a revelation, and exposure to "idle talk" that makes no sense. The mind is sometimes a battlefield where many battles are fought. There is a battle cry in the subconscious, existing but not felt.

The road a leader takes has to be straight and narrow with no blockades to obstruct his plan going in or out of any location. He must finish the race or the battle will be lost. If the battle should be lost in action or the mind, the vicious circle will claim its victim.

Barack's theory is being victimized, and the wolves want to sacrifice it in a vicissitude of changes. Changes that will feed their hungry desire for power.

Wolves hunt and pursue their game. They search through a region carefully, and they have no mercy on their prey. The desire and craving for food cause weakness.

This weakness is being displayed by all the opposers of the theory Barack has carefully laid out and wants to enforce for the American people. The solution is not perfect, but their solution is far from improving the economic problems.

To make improvements there has to be a change or addition that will increase the value of the failing conditions. Barack offered change, and change is exactly what his theory contains. The contents include the promises he spoke about on the campaign trail. Not all the promises can be fulfilled at one time.

The American people saw the better road and set off to balance the distance of a more excellent way concerning the position and condition that will increase progress, but there is a possibility the road may be rough and bumpy.

Barack has had a bumpy and dangerous course for months, and the roadbed is in constant question to be repaired. Repairing may satisfy or bring compensation to those who feel wronged. They seek to change Americans' minds about the theory presented by our new president.

Success is the only favorable outcome that will hush all the negative opposition coming against a negotiable peace treaty that would get past all the sharp curves, which are a hindrance to an earnest effort.

Barack's energy endures the endways to stop the hostile force, and he is eager to enervate the strength of the remarks by directing the gunfire at the harmful, viewless opinions.

The violence may be a violent blow caused by very strong feelings or actions. The pain can be severe and extreme, needing release. Sometimes feelings are tender and are prone to wipe out the damage that caused a wound.

A wound can be caused by cutting, stabbing, shooting, or any act harming a person in some way. Unkind words can injure feelings or one's reputation, or actions can cause an injury that is beyond a cure.

Barack has been shot at more than anyone can imagine and still be standing strong. He is strong-minded and has a strong-arm for self-defense. His attitude blocks the bullets and halts the control of the movement in the mechanism, preventing any injury that would occur.

The attacks on Barack and his theory will fail, simply because he is a fighter and knows that in combat one fights until one wins. He didn't want this dispute; he only wanted unity to heal this nation that is divided.

A divided house cannot stand, and a divided nation is in danger of being destroyed. America's enemies are lying in wait for the right opportunity to strike once again upon an unsuspecting nation that only knows how to quarrel and fight among themselves.

Iran has a theory, and it includes missiles that will wipe Israel off the map. This country wants to rule the world and be a super powerhouse, controlling the Middle East. This means getting rid of the Jews and possibly America.

America and Israel are peace-loving countries, and Iran knows by convincing the United States they only build missiles for use in their country, the method of producing weapons of mass destruction will be hidden until the right time to strike.

These foreign countries attack one another causing billions in damage. The tab of rebuilding is picked up by America, which can't afford to rebuild its own country. When will America wise up to the fact we can't support the whole world and survive as a nation.

A survivor can see their mistakes, correct them, and be suspicious of others' actions; not one foreign country is above suspicion. A survivor can continue to exist only if the plans and steps he takes are more advanced than the enemies.

The enemy America is fighting is brutal and has no regard for human life, not even their own. It is a spirit of hate that dwells deep in their mind infecting their heart and feelings.

This infection can spread from one to the other and one country to another country, causing an infectious disease called war; it can become red hot from exposure.

The exposure can lay open or uncover an open field allowing the enemies' gunfire because of foolish actions. America should investigate the plot, reveal the weapons, and destroy all of their artillery used to fight and murder.

America is fighting a war in its own government, and it is defeating the very purpose of turning the page forward, to go backward only means a defeated plan and a lost political system.

One day America's government will wake up to the fact it is not superhuman and, if it is not too late, begin to pick up the pieces of a shattered economy ruined because of war.

War has to be hell here on earth, always looking behind you and around the corner for the next enemy ready to blow himself and others into a million pieces.

Some people may say that war is the enemy itself—always popping up in unexpected places, sneaking up like a cat sneaks up on its prey, then attacks with a force that snuffs out the life of its victim.

A victim is unaware of his surroundings and completely trust his own instincts, not aware of the evil eye watching and ready to do harm. The evil mind is "wicked," "sly," and "cunning." In secret it is has a crafty way of deceiving others.

There is evil in greed. It is a green-eyed monster that loves wealth and will steal from a victim, even kill when necessary. They have a stealthy way to move secretly or quietly.

Bad mental activity can erupt like a volcano and expel actions done in secret, hidden from the views of man. The villainous state of one's mind is active with great wickedness.

This wickedness can work up a plan and operate in government unknown until it is revealed in some practical way. The workingman or woman has to pay the price of an administration that is graceless.

A government that has grace has favor, goodwill, mercy, and love for mankind. It will show a sense of what is right to prosper, having a courteous attitude to people of lower social positions.

A positive attitude doesn't criticize but offers help to increase progress. A positive manner can annoy unsure people. To them it is unwholesome, and they are not willing to consent to what they consider foolish.

Barack and his theory has been called foolish and wasteful spending. Critics call it insulting that he has backed away from his promises to the American people. As long as there are lawmakers, promises will be broken.

The most important concern Barack has at the present time is helping the economy get moving in a progressive direction. The method may not be persuasive to everyone or refer to their belief of change for America.

America needs an attitude change and start supporting Barack. He alone cannot bring change to a failing economy when the circumstances involve the whole world. Instead of criticism the House and Congress need lessons in their way of thinking.

The atrocity should stop and without delay to repair and heal the image a government needs to be successful in making decisions with a decisive character.

A decisive character is special. It will distinguish one from others with a noticeable feature. It will stand out and attract attention to the quality that is impressive to another person.

Barack is sometimes called analytical. In other words he analyzes what everyone has to say. It distinguishes him from someone else. He is always anxious to get others' input into his decisions.

Decisions can disadvantage some conditions and spread rumors. Rumors can cause disloyalty and discontent with disagreeable opinions. Disappointment with a disagreeable person can separate the connection needed to sustain a theory.

Bad-tempered people quarrel and have disputes refusing to allow approval "to consent," to an action or some fact that has been said or supposed to happen. These kinds of people are not only hard to deal with but are doubtful in all social positions.

The fact is America is billions in debt at the taxpayers' expense. Americans all across the United States are unemployed and do not know what tomorrow may bring. There may not be a roof to sleep under or food to eat. People are not buying anything, forcing many businesses to go bankrupt. The stock market keeps dropping, and all America can hear on the news is negative information.

Barack is attempting to rebuild the American people's confidence to trust again the sliding economy and put their money into it with assurance and believe the "boldness" will be a payback.

Payback would be a sudden activity and increase business, prices, value of property, a rapid growth in the economy showing positive results. People would spend again with no thought of losing their savings or retirement.

People who work and earn their retirement should be able to retire with the confidence of a safe fund to last their lifetime for their enjoyment and not have to worry about losing their wealth.

Wealth can be a strange thing. Some people have it, and others seek after it. It can make a person or break a person. Some people horde it, and others are free spenders that don't worry about tomorrow or care what the future may hold. A spendthrift will waste money and exhaust an inheritance.

Barack wants to create an America where every single person has the advantage of a good education. A college education is needful in today's world of new technology. Technology known today was not available a year ago. Knowledge is being increased, and who knows what tomorrow may bring.

People who want a college education should have the opportunity and funds in order to advance their mind to make a quality life for themselves and their family. Most good paying jobs require a college degree.

America knew that Barack would not be able to enforce every single part of his theory but believed he was honest in wanting to get what he could do for the American people who put their trust in him. He has proven that he wants to keep the confidence flowing toward a new tomorrow.

A tomorrow flowing with milk and honey, prosperity, peace, and happiness. All the elements where one can live and thrive. A successful life does not come easy. It takes hard work and a determination of the mind to will it. The power of the mind will decide what course to take in life.

Some people go through life without a purpose, depending on welfare and food stamps. Many are homeless, living in makeshift, homeless camps. Some of them refuse to work; others can't find a job they are qualified for.

A number of adult children live with their parents or sell drugs to survive. Drugs have become rampant in the United States ruining the lives of America's young people. Parents suffer with sorrow in distressful, troubled conditions of children hooked on drugs.

Barack's theory wants change in the way children live, seeks to remove drugs from America's streets where one can buy any form one's heart desires. Drugs is a way one escapes "reality" and feels safe in a world to them is hostile.

Change will keep teachers in schools, teaching children how drugs affect their health and how to say no when approached by a drug dealer. The dealer sometimes is a child or a parent that has been sucked into this wave of crime.

Crime leads to punishment, reform school, or prison, putting a mark on one's reputation for a lifetime. A marked person has a stain like crimson that will pop up on every application for a job.

Employment will help the problem concerning drugs, but it will not abolish the nature of the difficult problem. Therapy is needed in most cases, yet some people return to the same destructive habits that rob them of a progressive treatment.

America's government needs therapy to rid of all the corruption, fraud, and greediness possessing it and taking control in a direction restraining a recovery.

Greed in a way can be called a drug habit. It can grasp tightly, snatching the power to resist wanting things that one cannot afford to buy with upright means. Wanting too much is psychological. People who have this nature needs psychoanalysis to discover the underlying mental causes.

Mental illness is becoming a public concern to people as a whole. The soul or mind becomes diseased to the point of possessing a person's mind or personality. Psychology tries to explain why people act, think, and feel the way they do.

Barack's administration has uncovered a great deal of the corruption in government, some of it by the Republicans that want a fast comeback, but attacking Barack makes a comeback less likely. The American people are fed up with the quarrel going on within the most powerful government in the world.

The American people can imagine other countries, such as Iran, laughing and poking fun at a free democracy. America's government should prove and establish truth of all public demonstrations concerning the welfare of America.

To demoralize a country weakens the spirit and disheartens a people concerned with the way their country is treated. Every step to repair it should display strength in democratic ways.

A good society is always in pursuit of interests that benefit the United States. The challenges will confront a nation deep rooted in tradition. America is obligated, as a nation, to act for the people's best interest.

The best interest for a crippled nation, first and foremost, is safety—a prosperous economy treating all classes of people equal, recognizing problems directly affecting a global crisis, and solving all matters in a respectful style.

Danger of freedom being taken away from this great nation is constantly clawing at hearts and minds, bringing a realization that it can be snatched away in an instant moment. A peaceful, relaxed nation is a target for foreign countries to pounce upon with their claws like a bird seizes its prey.

All the peace talks in the world will not stop power-hungry countries from wanting to be number one; building missiles will always be a threat. Dictators who want control are going to intimidate Israel and America making it impossible to live in complete rest.

Talk is cheap and can deceive the most intellectual person in a government position. The slyness can steal one's judgment with great swelling words to entice by arousing hopes for a peaceful world.

There is an evil force that surrounds the Middle East, and it started in ancient times. The demons will not let go of a land belonging to the Jews. Some people wonder why such a tiny country is constantly fought over. The answer is evil is fighting good and evil wants to win.

There will be wars and rumors of wars until the end of time. One can only hope America is prepared and does not become disadvantaged in an unfavorable condition. A disaster will discredit the belief in the government's ability to protect against foreign warfare.

Good will always triumph over evil even though evil seems to win in certain areas of one's life, sometimes making the quality of life depend on lifesaving means. Some people say life is what you make it.

People who go in debt over their heads are asking for problems. They could lose their job, unexpected sickness could occur, an accident that causes one to be laid off for months, or any possible event can happen.

Barack is giving people a second chance with his stimulus bill. It will help people stay in their homes. It helps banks make loans to those that need a home or an automobile. It is supposed to help the uninsured get health insurance.

The plan is a good one; and if it works, if the deficit is cut, Barack will be considered one of the greatest presidents in the history of the United States; and the Republicans will have to give up their plan of attacks. These attacks are cunning and promote a slyness in getting what one wants.

Republicans want to be in charge. They fire at Democrats, creating an all-out battle. The battle is fought in the House and Congress while the American people watch and listen with helpless disapproval.

The people of America voted Barack into office, and he deserves to make his case with or without approval from all the opposers that wish him ill will. If his theory works, America will thrive once again; if it fails, so what. The Republican's theory didn't work either.

Hope for America and the future lie in Barack's theory. If it fails, he will try a new technique. We have to believe, have faith, and most important pray for him and his theory.

Prayer is the answer to many of this country's problems. It can open shut doors and make impossible dreams come true, take a sad situation and turn it into a joyous occasion. Prayer can bring relationships to a point of happiness and give it lasting peace. Life without God is death without hope for tomorrow.

There is not a perfect theory created by a human, but God in all his glory created "the perfect theory," and it includes all his elect he chose before the world was created. It will be a life free from war. Abundant love will exist forever and the "honor" of living with the "Creator" forever and ever.

This hope lives in every heart of a Christian and can never be taken away. Hope creates an active strength that endures the storms of life. A violent storm can blow a person's house away, but the force of hope is permanent.

All the material things in the world cannot compare with the glorious things God has prepared for his elect. Things on earth will vanish with death, but the things in heaven are eternal. Death brings decay to one's body, but the spirit never dies.

The spirit is created by God and lives in a body for the purpose of this created earth. At death the spirit leaves the body and returns to God who created all things for his pleasure. The world, people, and even world governments please God.

Sin and disobedience are two factors that give God dissatisfaction. People are born into sin and sin until death. This is why God sent his only son, Jesus, to be a "sacrifice" to save his people from their sins.

Jesus was the perfect offering to "God the Father" for the sins of an undeserving people. Jesus had a mission to carry out here on earth. He defeated Satan's warfare by doing good and dying on the cross. He now has victory, and he is at the right hand side of his father making intercession for all of the elect.

God's theory brings us back to Barack's earthly, imperfect plan for all Americans. Everyone wonders if it will work. Some people hope that it won't. It will work if God so wills it to be so simply because God's plan has an ending, and it will take place exactly at the time God set it before time began.

Barack's theory includes bringing back the American dream, which contains earthly possessions that can be taken away in an instant, by a storm, robbery, fire, or some means one is unable to control. Health care for all Americans can help control disease and sometimes cure an illness or disease, but it cannot cure sin or stop eventual death.

Death can occur in a split second, taking one into a supernatural and unknown place. One must and should be ready to look upon the face of one so powerful and wise—powerful because he is sovereign, wise because he knew everything before it began.

Wisdom comes from God. Having a relationship with the "Creator" can reveal very important facts that no one else can understand. These facts can lead one to certain heights never before experienced and can be very exciting.

Excitement can arouse one's feelings and produce magnetism to a certain thing or person. This excitement helped to get Barack elected as president. His speeches aroused good feelings in voters' minds, drawing them to him with his magnetic personality. His charm can "attract and influence" a person in mysterious, unexplained ways.

Charm has the power to take charge of a person or any situation. It can persuade by urging, arguing, or convincing a person in order to deal with undecided people. Some people are suspicious of a fast-talking persuasive manner of speaking and are not able to be won over. A person who has charm can be honest or deceiving, making it almost impossible to tell the difference.

Intellect combined with charm is twice as powerful in convincing even the smallest details to a person or group of persons. Intellect has all the facts down to a fraction while charm is an adoring personality, attracting one like a worm attracts a fish. There is an old saying, there are plenty of fish in the pond ready to be hooked.

An honest personality with charm is indeed hard to come by. Once found, it is amazing and strikes one with astonishment. A sudden burst of joy and surprise impacts one with delight, tempting the senses with a very pleasing touch, like a delicate fragrance awakens the sense of smell.

Barack has both of these qualities, intellect and charm. Most people say he is honest and up front with his ideas, plans, and promises. So far they are correct. He is keeping the promises he made to the American people. We just don't know yet if they will work.

The economy is still at the present time on a downhill. Jobs are still being lost by the thousands. Businesses and banks are going bankrupt, but we still have hope and faith that the future will shine with brightness.

A bright future depends on one man's plan, and the people supporting it. To support a plan, one has to believe in it that it will work, but fear has raised its ugly head preventing the economy to climb. Fear can paralyze one's thoughts and actions delaying a probable rebound.

Barack has said his plan needs time, but many people do not have time to wait. They have no job to go to, no money to spend, and many have no home to live in; but Barack has acted in a timely manner getting his plan through Congress. He knows that people are hurting, and it is a feeling he shares.

Being down and out often means pulling oneself up by one's bootstraps. Another old saying, sometimes it can be done alone, but most of the time one needs a push to help them realize being in a gutter where filth can bog one down is disgusting.

One can be helped out of the gutter, but it should be up to that person to stay out. One should realize one's mistake is enough to have gumption to carry on in a meaningful way in society. Common sense is a credit to one's ability to stay on a straight path.

Without a job a straight path looks crooked with sharp curves and hills that are hard to climb, giving one a sense of hopelessness. Barack is trying to straighten the path and bring back hope. Hope can turn the curves with ease and climb the hills with strength. Victory lies in four words, "I can do it."

Victory makes one proud of one's accomplishments, their ability to do a thing that has been a desire in one's heart for a long time. It gives a pleasing, relaxing feeling that can be enjoyed over and over in one's mind and life. To have victory one has to be determined, stay fixed on the aim, and reach the final goal.

Staying fixed on the aim is difficult for some people. A shy person is more likely to give up than an outgoing person. A shy person has issues he or she has to overcome. An outgoing person has a personality that drives them to be successful. They usually are determined and not easily deterred off course.

Issues a shy person has can be overcome if the person is willing. Sometimes help is needed. Shy people, in a way, are miserable, wanting to come out of their shell; but something inside will hold them captive. One has to learn to laugh at themselves and admit their faults.

A fault is an issue no one likes to admit to someone else, but it is necessary to build character. A know-it-all pretends to know everything not realizing the drastic impression he is making on other people. A clown thinks he has to make people laugh, and some clowns make good money as stand-up comedians, but some people are not as funny as they think they are. A boring person has no interest in exciting occasions and show no emotions.

Barack made the campaign trail, and his speeches were exciting. Some people fainted. There are not many people that has a positive effect on someone. The excitement stirred some people into action on his behalf, but a stirring can also produce negative actions in some responsive people.

People who have a responsive nature are easily moved and respond to feelings, words, or actions and sometimes embarrass themselves as well as others. People were moved by Barack's actions and words. The good news had a lot of meaning.

The good news, at present, is Barack is pushing his promises. One of them, to soon take place, is stem cell funding. Scientists can study cells for the purpose of finding cures for many diseases. Opponents believe it is immoral. This is a case that can be argued back and forth and still not be resolved.

A convincing case has to have facts and be free of doubt. If there is uncertainty in a situation, it can create anxious thoughts about the outcome. The consequence of making the wrong decision can overwhelm a case in progression.

One has to stay true to their beliefs. There are many different beliefs making it impossible to please everyone at the same time. Christians have different beliefs. Some believe they are right and all others are wrong. This is a fact that cannot be denied and is why there is so much controversy about opinions.

When you think about it, really deep down in your gut think it through, it would be a boring life if everyone thought the exact same way. Nothing in life would change, everyone would want the same things, believe alike, and wear the same clothes.

To live a boring life would be depressing causing one to have low spirits, decreasing one's vital activities. There would not be any excitement to arouse feelings of joy and happiness. Depression is a treatable condition, but a good mental attitude is a cure in itself.

Excitement is like an electric current passing from one's brain through their whole body. Some people get tingly feelings that explode into action. Shouting, crying, dancing, or running are a few of the emotions caused by excitement.

Sensitive people have a tendency to have hurt feelings very easily. They have strong sensitivity to words. This leaves little room to be honest in their presence. One has to watch what they say and always be apologetic of an offense.

Words can hurt or compliment a person. Hurt causes pain to one's ego. A compliment can build one up and give a person confidence in certain areas of their life or work. Kind words should be given freely at all times to all people, even if someone is considered to be an enemy.

An enemy hates and wants to harm another person. The reason can be because of jealousy. This envious condition can at times be dangerous. It can break up a marriage, cause suspicious behavior that needs watching, even commit murder. A kind word can sometimes win over an enemy.

Barack has used kind words, been apologetic, bent over backward to bring two different parties together on issues, and even entertained some of them at the White House. This conflict over issues is a difference of opinions.

Entertainment can reveal someone's character, reveal how one thinks, acts, and talks in private. An individual one-on-one connection is the best way to get to know someone's habits or faults. It probably would take more than one encounter.

A habit is often repeated by someone. Barack is a habitual person. He has a habitual smile, reads a great deal, and uses his blackberry quite often. All of these habits are good. Now what about bad habits. He surely has some for everyone does.

A faultfinder always finds fault with an idea or action, complains about imperfect conditions, and wants everything to be perfect. They are hard to please, convince, or persuade on important issues—wanting to argue their case, which in some circumstances can be the right course to take or can be circumstantial.

Circumstantial evidence is not important. It is a minor detail compared with the main fact. Main facts give the full details of an act or event proving them to be true. All the evidence brought against Barack was circumstantial, therefore not essential.

The circumstance the economy is portraying is real and true evidence. It keeps one wondering when will this slump end or will it ever. Barack has confidence that it will, depending on other factors, such as other countries taking action. He has hope we will get through these rough times.

Critics seem to think we won't get through this economic crisis. They say the new president has big ideas and too much spending that has shook the financial market into a sudden attack prolonging a rapid turnaround. Some optimistic critics think the crisis will end, but they don't know when or how.

When times are tough, it is hard to be optimistic. Human nature will act quickly and turn on the closest person available. Barack is getting his share of the blows, even getting accused of diverting attention to radio host Rush Limbaugh. Some people say Rush is wrong on most things he talks about. It is possible he will ruin the Republicans' chance of a comeback.

For a comeback, Republicans will have to be on their toes reaching for some hard facts to share with the American people; or Barack's theory will have to fail, a defeat they are hoping for. Republicans will have to get their act together and think about the American people instead of how to make themselves rich.

The American people want and deserve a life they can enjoy without the wealthy stealing it away. They deserve happiness that comes with a good job, a peace of mind that only good leadership can bring to the table. In all fairness they deserve to have health insurance that provides the same care the wealthy enjoy. The nest egg they build should not be disturbed and the eggs stolen.

A thief breaks in to rob and to kill, not caring that he is taking someone's life away. His thoughts are about self and what self wants no matter what the consequences of his actions. Most of the time he does not suffer from doing wrong.

Self is one's own person and cares about one's own interests. A selfish person always puts self first, being absorbed in his own thoughts and affairs. He is self-assertive, insisting on his own wishes or opinions. Sometimes he has no control over his actions. He loves self and cares about personal advantage.

Unselfish people are self-sacrificing and selfless. They are successful by their own efforts and have control over feelings and actions, asking for no help with their resources. They believe in their own ability and judgment in keeping their life in order.

To be successful one has to have a willing mind and the energy to see an idea through. Success comes through hard work, always pushing oneself toward their goal to finish the race with pride in one's wished-for ending.

Running a race takes an eagerness to win for a reason. The reason may be money, a prize, or for charity. The competition can be great. One needs to be in top physical condition. The first one to reach the finish line wins the expected prize.

The presidential race was run by several good candidates. They ran with a boldness in speed, but only one could win, and the race became a public show. The final two ran at high speeds, and they shifted gears often, but one was a speeder and came in first with high marks.

A public show tells the audience every detail of the presentation. Some details are positive, some are negative. Negative details come across as carelessness. Being careless in a public show can produce unfavorable results, therefore harming the show. Positive details present a well planned out public exhibition disclosing the facts.

An audience will grade the quality of the public show as either good, bad, or in between. If the show has positive results, it can appeal to one's emotions. Some people laugh, cry, or clap their hands applauding the first-class art of excellence. The clapping can be annoying if it is loud or constant.

America watched the public show concerning the presidential race and were held in high emotion as Obama, McCain, and Clinton laid out their planned details. The show was well planned, and each candidate had an enormous amount of support. The excitement escalated during and after each performance.

The theory each candidate presented to the public was both positive and negative. Some parts caused anger and distrust, but the positive parts brought forth good news to most people that were waiting for something to lift their spirits.

The good news, the majority of the public heard, was Barack Obama gave the best performance and had the more positive theory—a theory to help grief-stricken people and end a long drawn-out war, a war that has no mercy.

In order to give a good performance, one has to focus their attention on the script—each act and study the manuscript until it is memorized, practice until one is exhausted, and make certain it will please an audience. If an audience enjoys a play or event, one will know it by the applause.

Barack pleased an audience of millions that shouted, danced, and thanked God for his performance. To please an audience that huge, the exhaustion must have been overwhelming, but he never gave in to it or expressed any frustration during the event. He kelp his cool throughout the show, and it was to his favor. He was talented, and the people liked him very much.

Frustration will only make one feel worthless and defeated in any situation one may be engaged in. The puzzled mind can't seem to focus on important facts to remember. One may feel helpless and be confused as to what to do next. Confusion happens to many performers.

Though Barack Obama is an expert at many things, the negative rumors still float on deep waters; and the waves carry them out to sea throughout the earth, to be heard by all willing to listen. Negative rumors carry a message of disorder and strife.

Keeping order seems to be extremely difficult for people who don't want to follow rules. Rules are to be obeyed. They give the information one is to follow throughout life. To disobey rules, one is considered not well behaved. A person not well behaved will find themselves in trouble at school, work, etc., and most of the time blame someone else.

President Barack Obama also has rules and orders to follow. He doesn't have all the power. He made a lot of promises, and he is trying with all his power to keep them. He puts money where his mouth is, and it will take money to get America out of the mess currently making everyone so fidgety.

Fidgety people are nervous, uneasy about problems and conditions they have no control over. It causes concern from others about a situation that has not fully developed, prolonging the case. A case in question needs a lot of consideration to ease one's mind.

Idle talk that one hears about other people and their affairs is not always true. Gossipy persons are fond of repeating hearsay messages that only harms someone or a condition. There is not a way to stop gossip, but if one listens, one may be drawn into a web of deceit.

Deceit is sort of like a spider's web. One will be enticed by words and become tangled in a confused mass of false statements that is intended either to impress in conversation or harm someone's reputation. When engaging in this type of conversation, one should watch their words carefully or one may end up in a court of law.

A court of law is exactly the position Barack is in even though he is the head of the administration. Laws have to be voted on and passed by lawmakers. Barack is being judged very harshly in all his decisions and actions. His actions are being scrutinized daily. He has had to act promptly to try to rescue bad judgment in America's government.

Bad judgment and decisions has put America in a state of deep doubt. People doubt Barack and his stimulus plan. They doubt the economy will recover. There is doubt the war in Iraq and Afghanistan will ever end. Doubt floods newspapers and TV causing fears that make one tremble.

Doubt causes one to be uncertain and not sure of anything or anyone. This suspicious attitude always will raise questions concerning any person or event one does not understand. Doubting Thomas did not believe God raised Jesus from the grave until he saw for himself.

Thomas heard the words Jesus preached and heard him say he would be crucified and resurrected the third day, but still he doubted that a supernatural happening could occur. Humans doubt and it is unfortunate because faith can move mountains.

Faith will trust and have honest intentions. Loyal supporters are faithful of one they believe in and trust. They are open-minded and fair, not prejudiced. A person can be judged prematurely before all the facts are made known.

Faith in God is the key to trust. When one trusts God with his life, a whole new life begins with new attitudes and actions. One looks the same but feels completely different. Joy and happiness replaces sadness and gives one a new outlook on life. Others notice a difference they cannot describe. To trust God with your life means trusting him in death.

Jesus conquered Satan and took the sting out of death. A Christian no longer fears death, for to be absent from the body is to be present with the Lord. The Lord is coming back to earth to rule and to reign as King, the only King of the whole world.

There won't be any criticism or complaining, for Jesus will rule with a rod of iron. Every knee shall bow and confess that he is Lord. There won't be two different parties that argue among themselves, making the laws. There will be perfect peace, and this event is what Christians are eagerly waiting for.

Peace will dominate the world simply because Jesus has the victory, and the evil angel, Satan, will no longer be in the world to cause disorder and fear or worry about finances, sickness, or pain. Disease will have disappeared like the wind of a storm; then, the calmness appears out of nowhere.

Some people think it is a fairy tale. They believe it because they don't have faith or a relationship with God in prayer. Prayer can change one's outlook on life, create peace in one's mind and give energy to a body in pain. This is peace that passes all understanding.

An idle mind is the devil's workshop. He creates all different kinds of mischief in a mischievous mind to "promote" his desires. A creative mind, on the other hand, will "focus" on worthwhile projects to inspire oneself and others.

A psychologist can study the mind, but only God knows one's thoughts and intentions or what causes a mental disease. A psychopathic person is likely to become insane, not realizing right actions from wrong actions and require a person to be locked away in an insane institution.

The jobless rate is the worst it has been since the Great Depression, and many people have flipped their lid, either killing themselves or committing mass murder. These people are out of control concerning their feelings and actions, a behavior problem affecting many people in America. They believe nothing will change, that they have been done wrong and are doomed anyway, a lie straight from the devil's mouth.

Satan walks about seeking whom he may devour, and he devours people with mental and behavior problems. People who have these kind of problems need medical and spiritual help. Sometimes people need someone to talk to and reassure them that to be a responsible person you need to attack problems before they attack you.

The problems Barack is facing are enormous. He is attacking them with all the ammunition he has and trying to find a solution to the differences in opinions. Barack is a leader, and he will lead them to safety if they would be willing to follow.

Barack's hair is turning salt and pepper in color, but it is the least of his problems. He has a country on the brink of bankruptcy that needs a fix, millions of people in a frantic condition, attacks on his every move; but he knew all of this beforehand.

People worry about tomorrow, but tomorrow will take care of itself is an old saying that has proven to be true in many cases. Worry only causes uneasy feelings and annoy those who do not worry about problems, preferring instead to find a solution.

Solving a problem or problems take careful examination to determine the cause. Once determined, it has to be broken down into categorical arrangement to classify where the problem is taking one's mind and to be aware of each obstacle in one's path.

Barack was aware of all the problems in America that is causing the widespread havoc. He worked out his plan and put it in groups so the American people could understand the method to be used. Most Americans bought his plan, and now it is time to support it. If anyone has a better plan, it will surely make him happy.

American people are quick to pass judgment and complain because America has always been a land of opportunity, a land fortunate to be free from dictators that dictate and rule without the people's input.

Barack has invited everyone's input. It identifies him as a president and not a dictator or a socialist. He realizes the people are the government, and the people elected him to take care of the government's problems. Now is the time to stop all the rhetoric talk and use genuine words.

Genuine words are true, not imagined or made up and exist as a fact. Words that are true support a person and helps that person achieve the aim he has targeted, giving him victory and success in a plan of revival.

Revival is a plan America needs, not only physical but spiritual. Physical problems as well as spiritual problems are plaguing American people, and it is obvious throughout the world. Revival brings people together and conquers fear.

A disagreeable person is like a plague. He or she torments, annoys, and offends others with manners that are bothersome. These actions need to be brought under control by pointing out the words or manners that has become punishment to someone else.

Punishment is sometimes painful and is brought upon someone for a wrong that they have done. Opposers of Barack are using harsh words and insulting remarks to punish him for winning the presidency, not realizing they are in the wrong.

Children are taught right from wrong as soon as they are old enough to understand doing wrong will bring punishment. A few years ago, a belt could be used to discipline a child. Now it is child abuse. Children used to fear discipline, for they knew it hurt. Some parents think their children are perfect and can do no wrong.

The attitude parents have about their children's behavior has a great deal of influence on how their actions will manifest when they are adults. Parents sometimes wonder why their children get involved with drugs or prostitution. They should consider their own actions.

Children are often left alone to raise themselves while their parents work. A child cannot teach one's self, and it becomes a problem as an adult. Two paychecks are better than one and can buy material possessions, but children need their parent's guidance throughout their childhood.

A happy childhood is enjoyed when both parents are available to talk to about problems and give advice on difficult matters. Children need love and to be cared for above material wealth or what one wishes to do in their own life. One can never relive their childhood except in one's own imagination.

One can form pictures in one's mind and imagine a perfect childhood, but when love is absent, the pictures are fake. Children are fond of imagining; and some children imagine they are a movie star, a singer, artist, or whatever their dreams are when they grow up.

Some children form a picture of an imaginary friend in their mind and talk to the friend as if a friend really exists. A psychiatrist is quick to say this is normal behavior. Maybe it is. After all it is imaginary, and the friend only exists in the child's mind.

Barack formed a picture in his mind as a child of becoming president one day. In his imagination he was able to create new ideas and put them into practice. His picture and ideas became a reality that America will never forget and neither will he.

The picture Barack formed was also about plans and opinions that became so real in his mind that he put those plans and opinions to work in order to accomplish the exact picture he formed many years ago. That picture is now being seen all over the world today on TV, the Internet, and in books and magazines.

Forming pictures in your mind can be healthy but also immoral. Some people form pictures of robbery or murder, creating a life of crime that leads to being locked away, sometimes for life. A life of crime is a life without freedom.

Freedom is what America is all about—free to speak one's mind, free to choose a religion, free to vote and elect government officials, free to work and raise a family. America has liberty, and one can act or think as one pleases, but liberty is not to be taken for granted.

At a roundtable meeting, Barack said he knows people are confused about what he is trying to do, but he asked people to work with him to get the economy going again. The government officials at the table agreed that it is necessary, and they want to do it for the good of the country, a right attitude approached Barack and he looked pleased.

Working together is what Barack has wanted throughout the campaign and his presidency. It takes unity to stay on main issues, solve problems in America, work with other countries to solve world problems that hinders every chance of a recovery.

World problems are a huge concern for every country because of hunger, unclean air, homelessness, and war. The threat of war is always present in everyone's mind. War is ugly, and it takes innocent lives. An attack requires retaliation.

One good thing came out of the Iraq war. It set the Iraqi people free from a horrible dictator; they now have their own government and are free to vote. The Iraqi people are now free, but the American military has not been set free to return to a normal life.

Barack has promised to end the war in Iraq and concentrate on winning in Afghanistan. This is a war that may never end unless America has help from other countries to fight terror that seems to spread like wildfire, burning whatever lies in its path.

Terror is a monster to be reckoned with. This huge creature is too wicked to be human and is extremely shocking. The dreadful monstrosity has to be destroyed. The truth is, it is hard to kill. It keeps hiding in unknown places, sneaks around to prey on unsuspecting victims.

Bravery does not hide. The U.S. military has courage, and they face this monster whenever they can seek it out of the caves and hideouts where it dwells in a cowardly condition. The U.S. military bravely goes where many people would not dare to take a chance on losing their life.

America has to decide if the Communist countries are supportive of fighting terror. Without their help it will be a hard task because terror can hide in these countries. Terror hides in safe places, and it includes the United States.

Barack has repeated the remark that the Iraq war was a distraction from the war in Afghanistan. The Iraq war brought terrorists from other countries to blow themselves and others up with homemade bombs. These terrorists have no mercy, and they use women and children to hide behind.

A coward will kill themselves because they cannot face the fact of not having victory or facing someone with fair intentions. They want the satisfaction of taking others out with them. If they would be honest, they would admit their fear of the U.S. military.

The last war to be fought on earth will be between Jesus and Satan, good and evil. Satan cannot win. He only has the power that God will give him. Jesus is God and has all power. He will win and have the victory over evil. Evil will vanish into the pit where it belongs and will never be seen again.

In the mist of trials and troubles, it is a comfort to know Jesus is coming to end all wars and bring peace to a people waiting for his return, a return sure to happen sometime in the future. No one but "God the Father" knows the hour or the day.

God is a spirit. Humans are made in his image. There has to be a resemblance of some sort. One thing for sure, he knew exactly what he was doing. Man tries to design a body and has come a long way, but man cannot create a spirit that lives within a body.

A person's spirit is the real person. He or she may not want to admit it, maybe because they don't understand it. If they did, there would be no suicide for one is not killing oneself, only their body. One's spirit will return to God to be judged.

God's judgment will be fair. He is holy and just. No one on earth can look upon his face and live; his glory is too great. He will not share his glory with anyone. Satan tries but he is doomed to a death that never ends.

The promises of God will be kept even though they are criticized by people who do not know God or understand the words that he gave to his prophets and disciples. They will miss out on the greatest event ever to take place in history, an event so thrilling one will tremble with excitement.

Barack becoming president was a great event, but it won't be the greatest. There is one coming who has a more powerful speech and will be able to inspire with words never before heard. These words will touch one's heart with a burning desire to be like him.

When Jesus appears, all Christians will be like him, for they have given him their heart, a heart of stone now changed to follow him and obeys his commands. Commands that are not hard to follow as some people believe but are as easy as breathing air.

Air is precious, and man has polluted it with all the inventions over the years. The automobile, airplanes, rockets, all of them put out a poisonous exhaust that is harmful to the air that one breathes. Clean air is a part in Barack's theory.

There is hope and faith in the theory Barack has presented to the American people and the government officials. Without this theory or it working, hope and faith will turn to despair, a hopeless feeling that the economy or their lives will never get any better.

Barack wants to turn America back toward the "American Dream"—toward a tomorrow filled with the wealth it once had, a place where children don't have to worry about a job or college, money for food, a car, or a safe and comfortable world to live in.

Some people say it will take a miracle and maybe it will, but it won't be Barack's magic. If it happens, it will be by God's power. If Barack's theory works, it will be because God gave him the inspiration and the willingness to present it.

Miracles do happen today. Some people deny they exist and believe they left when the disciples died, which is not true. Jesus said to ask that it may be given to you. If you believe Jesus, you can receive a miracle. People without patience give up easy and go through life being defeated.

Defeat will keep a person and a country from receiving what God wants to give. God is generous and pours out blessings on the "good" and the "evil," blessings that none really deserves. But God is good and has pity for his creation. He desires fellowship with people, many who don't even give him a thought. His spirit will not always strive with man.

The "American Dream" involves God. Without him, there would not be an economy to rescue, air to breathe, water to drink, animals to save, food to eat, homes to live in, money to buy material things, children to raise, and last but not least there wouldn't be an earth or people.

PART 9

THE AMERICAN DREAM

As Americans, we must believe in the American Dream and pull together, not fight as the immature do when unforeseen misfortune happens. Immature people cannot function well because their seeing is not believing.

The American Dream can once again become a reality. It will take hard work and sacrifice, not judging facts or spreading false rumors. Rumors become worse as they are passed from one to the other.

This dream must include education for our children and our grandchildren, a good economy that prospers where we, our children, and their children can grow old with enough retirement funds to live comfortably.

Included in this dream are plenty of jobs, no layoffs that rob people of their homes, health insurance, and many times their very own dignity.

There is freedom from war and strife, a calmness of order and security. This stillness will quiet one's very soul and inspire the healthy power to produce strength in one's abilities.

These abilities are possessed by many educated and noneducated persons, some special skill or talent, such as music, singing, or writing poetry. An orator has the skill to speak well in public.

Barack often spoke of the American Dream in his speeches and how it is slowly coming to an end without some changes. The greatest country on earth needs a change from the hugger-mugger conditions that exist.

Conditions that require reexamination of rank, social positions, and special work. We must exercise our muscles in expressing dependence on a better method. There should be a methodical, systematic, orderly way of deciding on any solution that is causing madness and anger to develop.

The unfolding of a plan takes time, requires patience, a willingness to endure without complaining or losing self-control. Self-examination of one's conduct and motives can be self-filling and lead to containing oneself.

Self-interest is selfish and cares little for the welfare of others, insisting on one's own wishes and opinions. These assertive people are occupied with their own interests and affairs. They do not have the knowledge of themselves or care about pleasing others.

Barack's plan should help in many ways to bring America back into the fold, bringing together the necessary parts to close the hollow place that has become a valley and made the "American Dream" worthless.

America is worthy and deserves the wealth that so many Americans are able to enjoy. This national disaster can and must be repaired, put in a position favorable to even the opponents.

When one thinks of the "American Dream," they sometimes think it is unreal or impractical and in a vague way wonder if it only exists in the imagination. Though we form beautiful pictures in our minds, they can create new ideas. We can put them into practice to follow in action and to do the process well. In time the course or condition will be finished, polished, and perfected.

Excellence is completely skilled, having all of its parts. Nothing can be broken or missing. It is faultless, without defect. It has the utmost exactness. This requires making severe demands often causing results that are not predicted.

America once had pleasure in this "American Dream" that seems to have passed from existence and be lost from sight, but it is not invisible to the sightseer. It is alive in the heart of every American and will never die.

This dream Barack so well spoke about can once again "arouse and excite" the ones who believe that laws protect the enjoyment of one's rights, the justice and fair treatment everyone deserves. It can excel surpassing all others.

The determination Barack has displayed in keeping his promises, one can assume he is trying to settle his mission beyond question. The misfortune America has experienced is a debt made by bad decisions. Good judgment is needed to form opinions without condemnation. Barack has a firm and clear view of the judgment he wants a resolution for.

The "American Dream" is not imaginary. It is an existing fact and genuine. We have a clear understanding and full awareness that it is possible to realize that dreams do come true.

To work toward a dream is to put it into operation. The effort will assist the engineering structure. Work out a plan and develop it. Study the outlines of the subject and obey the rules. Practice a practical method of procedure and in the process of time the dream will move forward.

When a dream or idea comes true, it becomes living proof or evidence that the effort and plan grew out of a mindful eye having imagination and the result is a constant reminder.

All Christians have a dream that they know in their hearts will come true in God's divine timing. God planned this dream before time began, and it includes all of his elect people. His plan is perfect, and no one can stop this dream from becoming reality.

All Christians are coheirs with Jesus to inherit all things, even eternal life. Many people believe at death life ends. It would be tragic since life is like a vapor. Life will pass quickly, and without God, hope and dreams will pass too.

PART 10

THE FIRST LADY

Michelle Obama is a woman of elegance and known as a lady of fashion. She often wears sleeveless dresses and wore a black sleeveless dress for her White House picture.

Michelle loves her husband, President Barack Obama, with "passion," which is not often seen in the White House. She blew him a kiss during his speech to Congress. She is a woman who knows what she wants and is protective of Barack and their two daughters, Malia and Sasha.

The first lady will grace the White House not only in appearance but with a style and characteristic that distinguishes her as very special. The qualities she possess is "generous giving" and help to "poor and suffering" people. She works with various charities and has love for fellow men and women, showing a pleasant and agreeable nature.

Michelle will no doubt draw attention throughout the world as having a powerful leadership in many areas. Throughout the campaign she presented "spectacular" speeches and touched many hearts.

She was criticized for the remark, "This is the first time that I have ever been proud of America." She was able to silence the comment and win Americans over in a noble manner. Being noble herself, she will walk in total magnificent splendor.

This journey will be an enduring but rewarding experience, taking her on many adventures where an accomplished lady with grace skillfully "succeeds" in completing the mission before her.

Her beautiful face will appear in newspapers, books, on magazine covers, and be a feature attracting attention in all the world for the human race to adore.

She will be loved by whites and blacks throughout the administration. She is already drawing much publication and admiration. She is admired greatly for the way she selects her wardrobe and has favorable results. The news has said she may even start her own line of clothing.

There is not a "task or force" that can come against her faithfulness to be true to herself or to others. The strength and self-control she possesses can maintain any possibility. This lady will be the rock that holds the family in the right position for any unfolding problems.

Michelle and her family will adorn the White House as no other family has historically. The history she and Barack made together are events that are important and systematic. This delightful family has an orderly way of planning and a system of facts. This audacious lady calls the White House the people's house and recently invited a group of students to come and taught them about the history of the White House, Lincoln, and the slaves.

The first lady will experience an enormous amount of pain because of the bitter criticism of her African American husband becoming president, but she surely knows that President Lincoln also was bitterly criticized. Having a high intellect, she understands and will maintain the onward course of her duties.

These duties require being a helpmate in the presidency and giving speeches at important events. She may travel to foreign countries for various reasons. Whatever her duties may be or wherever they take her, there will be a binding force of submission. Michelle is adjusting quite well to the White House duties according to what people are saying, and she has to be mindful of every step she takes, giving heed to advice. Well-informed people make wise, sensible, and thought-out plans.

This unlikely dream is not just President Barack's but is shared by Michelle, the unreal, impractical but ideal place that only a few can imagine. It is a dream come true, no more distant, faraway space to hide with unlimited room. It is a space that can now be occupied by a dreamer looking for a plan.

Michelle will work hard in the real world and will make her husband proud. America will share in the gratifying period marking such a historical present and remember that defining moment in history that shook the world and made a difference. America will never forget the momentous decision made in our election.

The world is no more white and black but in living color. A distinguishing quality shows who one really is and declares one's opinions or plans. America is no more color-blind but able to see vivid privileges between members of the white and black races.

Hope produces faith, and faith produces trust. Only the faithful keep their promises. A person who is honest and loyal has no intent to deceive. Deceivers are fake. The deception soon becomes public knowledge. Hope and faith were on America's mind when this new president and Michelle took office.

They had a plan of change that was well presented, seemed well thought-out to bring useful results needed to obtain a resurrection and restore to life an economy slowly dying. This world crisis is a danger to their dream, bringing into existence the true state of actual affairs and dangers they must face. It is a genuine consciousness that without reality destruction can present itself without delay. A revival from decay would provide a different outlook and restrain the loss of power.

Michelle is the backbone that will help Barack and support him on all sides, even the front line. She will help shield him from the darts that move swiftly and sting as they enter his flesh drawing blood. She is the love of his life. He made that clear to all America.

www.ingramcontent.com/pod-product-compliance
Lightning Source LLC
Chambersburg PA
CBHW031300280526
45784CB00004B/1930